I LIGNMENT

ILIGNMENT

PERSONAL
TRANSFORMATION
"RE-ALIGNMENT"
AND
GROWTH

...

THE JOURNEY TO CREATE
YOUR GREATEST LIFE
FROM THE INSIDE OUT

RON MANSETH

CREATIVITY
EMPOWERED
PRODUCTIONS

Published by Creativity Empowered Productions
info@creativityempowered.com

Copyediting by James Gallagher

Cover Design by Rizwana Kausar

Book Design & Publishing by Kory Kirby
SET IN SABON LT PRO

ISBN 979-8-9856753-4-4 (hardback)
ISBN 979-8-9856753-3-7 (paperback)
ISBN 979-8-9856753-5-1 (eBook)

Printed in the United States of America

CONTENTS

PART FOUR: CREATING A NEW WORLD

PART FIVE: YOUR TRANSFORMATION JOURNEY   **237**

APPENDIX

MY LIFE'S PURPOSE

I Help People Realize Their Greatest Life ...

to "Be Free—Live Free—Work Free"

Once I discovered my Inner Purpose, my life finally made sense! As you discover your True Purpose, it, too, will bring your life into sharp focus and will empower you to be all you were destined to become!

I wrote I-Lignment to be a catalyst for you to discover your Greatest Life ... a life that lies inside you, patiently waiting to be uncovered and discovered.

I'll do whatever I can to be there for you as you take this I-Lignment journey!

— Ron Manseth

THE JOURNEY

I, LIKE YOU, have been on a journey through life, with ups and downs, twists and turns, with all its opportunity as well as unpredictability, inconsistencies, conflicts, and dysfunction. However, my life has been good overall, with many great relationships, experiences, adventures, and successes. I have been living what appeared to be a successful life.

But there always seemed to be something missing. There was this inner sense of emptiness and dissatisfaction. I felt that something in me was incomplete. I was constantly thinking of where I could be that would be better than where I was. I found myself having inappropriately strong reactions to something someone would say or to something that happened. With constant change happening all around me in the world and all the opportunity and choices available to me, making definitive decisions was sometimes difficult. Many times, fear and anxiety surrounded decisions, causing me to not decide.

I wanted to do something to make things better and fill

the void I felt on the inside. I knew I could be living life better . . . but I didn't know how.

PROFOUND SHIFTS . . . THAT TRANSFORMED MY LIFE

In my latter twenties, I began my personal journey to understand life and how life could be lived more powerfully. Over time, I realized I wasn't living life consciously. This came to me in a series of profound personal experiences and discoveries that occurred over several decades.

Throughout this book and at the appropriate times, I'll describe the "aha" shifts in awareness that led to my personal transformation and inspired me to write this book. The relevance of these profound shifts, as they apply to your life, will become evident.

Right now, I'll share only four of the shifts that kept me searching for more and led me to the truth of life.

FIRST PROFOUND SHIFT: I'M NOT A MANUFACTURED IDENTITY!

When I started digging into my life in my latter twenties, I first reflected on my life to that point.

I remembered, in my teen years, that I didn't want to have an identity manufactured by someone else. It didn't feel authentic. I wanted to be unique, to be myself. This desire showed up in my teen life in different ways. I tried to always think through the appropriate response to people or an event and not just go along with the crowd. Many times, I didn't look at myself in the mirror because I didn't want to be egotistical, focused just on me. I avoided wearing clothes with the brand printed on them; I didn't want to be identified with a label. My focus was predominantly on others and on seeing what I could do to bring happiness and love into their lives. I realized later how intuitive and prophetic these acts were at a young age. This was the first of four profound shifts.

I was now looking at life differently than most others. I increased my focus on self-improvement in high school and then college. Because of this focus, the feelings of inadequacy, both internal and external, became amplified. I didn't feel "good enough." I wanted to change and improve my life but was unaware of any true, inspiring guide/coach with a clear path for personal transformation. So, instead, I went down my own path of improving myself based on the example of others who had achieved "success" in the world.

Even though my intent was not to manufacture an identity, I was manufacturing one based on external input from what appeared to be successful people. I got a degree in structural engineering with a minor in business and entrepreneurship.

I launched my professional life, first running a small business in San Diego. Then, after pursuing a master's in information systems, I joined IBM as an account sales executive. I attained success by external standards. My knowledge and experience grew. I consistently achieved my sales quotas. My bank account and investments were growing significantly. I got married. We bought a house. We had a great group of friends and were constantly busy entertaining or traveling to exciting destinations.

Despite my apparent success, I was always thinking about being somewhere else . . . somewhere better than where I was. I felt the urge to constantly improve, to fill the lack I felt within me, and to meet the unmet expectations of others.

What led up to the next profound shift happened,

interestingly, after one of my big successes at IBM, when I was twenty-nine. I was leading a project to win back the high-tech engineering design and manufacturing business at one of our large customers in San Diego. Our state-of-the-art, $15 million solution was complex and required a substantial effort from a large worldwide team. We were successful! I received recognition and financial rewards. What surprised me, however, was how empty the recognition and rewards felt. I loved the intrinsic feelings of satisfaction while working collaboratively with the IBM team and the customer, leading up to the final win. But the letdown and emptiness I felt afterward surprised me.

All the effort to form who I was at that point in my life didn't lead to a deep sense of happiness. I felt empty. The sense something was missing was strong. I was getting my sense of self-worth from an inauthentic, manufactured identity. I felt like I was skimming the surface of life . . . that there was something missing at a much deeper level—something more meaningful and authentic.

SECOND PROFOUND SHIFT: I REALIZED THE JOURNEY IS INWARD . . . NOT OUT THERE

I realized the journey needed to be inward and personal; the destination where authenticity and meaning were to be found was not out there somewhere. It was to be found within.

I felt empowered because, if the journey is inward, I could make it happen independent of others. I wasn't a victim. I was now in charge of making the changes in my life, and it was up to me and me alone. This was a huge revelation.

Now the question was how. My journey to find out was

launched . . . without a road map. I became a voracious reader of books on personal development, psychology, and professional development, and I attended many workshops and retreats. I attended the Presbyterian church as well as the Self-Realization Fellowship (my first introduction to Eastern spirituality).

My perspective began to shift through all my reading and experiences. I started feeling separate from my manufactured identity. But I still didn't understand who I was apart from that identity. I continued the search for the real me.

As so many people experience, especially without a road map for guidance, my personal growth over the next twenty years came in spurts. I had periods when I felt I was progressing rapidly, only to be followed by periods when I felt I was regressing, caught up in the world of inauthenticity.

However, my relentless desire and focus on personal transformation led to the discovery and accumulation of simple and powerful truths of life. Each one I applied to my own life with positive impact. As each was added, they had an accumulative, holistic, positive effect.

THIRD PROFOUND SHIFT: I EMBRACED UNCONDITIONAL LOVE AS THE MOST LIFE-CHANGING EXPERIENCE

The third profound shift came during a turbulent time in my life.

When the 2009 recession hit, I was involved in real estate investing and financing as a career. The recession hit me hard. My ability to make money in real estate came to a screeching halt; our house tanked in value, causing us to have to short sale; my wife and I got divorced. My net worth went from well over a million dollars to zero in a short period of time. My dad was diagnosed with dementia, later Parkinson's, and we had to move him out of our childhood home into an assisted-living facility. I became his guardian. My mom had a stroke. Both my mom and dad eventually passed away, along with twenty-three friends and family members over a six-year period. My life was unrecognizable.

Fortunately, I knew by then that life brings you what you need for your higher good . . . although I have to admit, it wasn't all that clear at the time. I had wanted to formally become a professional life coach, even though I had been informally coaching people for most of my life and saw this as being an opportune moment to do so. As I went through formal coaching training, I became my "first client."

This led to my third profound and most life-changing shift. I'd been deeply working on myself in a personal retreat for several weeks. The day the profound moment happened, I had been releasing many things that had built up over my lifetime. In an instant, everything disappeared. Everything around me disappeared. I disappeared. The only thing that remained was unconditional love. I started crying from joy and said out loud, "This is it!" This incredible moment I knew to be the truth.

Something we spend a lifetime looking for out there from others is, in truth, inside us already, at the core of who we are. We are, at our core, unconditional love. Having this experience of your innermost self, at your very core, is the most incredible experience you'll ever have . . . absolutely life-changing.

FOURTH PROFOUND SHIFT: I FOUND A NEW, POWERFUL MODEL FOR TRANSFORMATION

After this experience, I doubled down on coaching and made a personal commitment to find the most powerful, yet simple, path to personal transformation.

I continued my search but from a different state of mind. I knew what was possible and where to find it . . . it was inside me and all of us, not out there somewhere. Through the process of working on myself and with other clients over the ensuing years, as well as learning from new and powerful life experiences, the transformation approach and model came as a revelation . . . the I-Model and I-Lignment.

I have applied them to my own life, in coaching others, and I'm now sharing them with you to help you live the life you've always dreamed of.

NOW BEGINS YOUR TRANSFORMATION . . .

I'm so excited this book was drawn to you. It found you for a reason. This is the beginning of your journey to who you really are . . . who you are authentically and powerfully . . . and it will help you realize a life beyond your wildest dreams! The book will guide you through an understanding of why your life is as it is . . . and then will assist you to discover the greatness that lies within you . . . waiting to be released . . . waiting to be lived.

It's important you read through the entire book to understand the holistic ("whole"-istic) nature of the transformative approach and to receive its full benefit. Also, suspend judgment as you read the book . . . read everything as if it's the first time you've heard it. If you do, it will have maximum potential of transforming your life! You'll awaken to a whole new way of living life that will bring a passion for life . . . unlimited, unconditional love . . . a deep sense of peace . . . infinite joy . . . personal freedom . . . true power . . . and an uncovering of your True Purpose!

YOUR INTENTION . . .

It's important you create an intention for reading this book. A heartfelt intention will put power behind your reading and will tap into an inner source of insight and wisdom. It'll also be the catalyst for taking right action.

Your intention may look something like this: *"I'm fully open to discovering a new way to transform my life . . . allowing me to be in and live from my inner greatness."* Create it from deep within yourself. Make it your own. Make your intention so powerful it motivates you to greatness. Always keep it in mind as we embark on this journey together.

I want to let you know I will, unapologetically, be using many metaphors related to nature throughout the book. I was raised and live in the Pacific Northwest, which I love. The natural beauty and richness of this area is unparalleled. I've developed a strong connection with nature. It's a powerful teacher of life lessons. It remains my main source of inspiration and connection to the truth of life.

I wish you all the best in your life journey. I'm incredibly grateful to be part of your journey and to bring you a new, powerful perspective that will propel you to living a life you've only imagined.

Sending you unconditional love always,
–*Ron*

PART ONE:
WAKING UP TO
A NEW WAY
OF LIFE

CHAPTER ONE:

"I"

WHO AM "I"?

We've all asked this question at various times in our lives. You may be asking this question of yourself right now. This is one of the most fundamental inquiries of human existence . . . and has been asked for eons.

You could be drawn to this question because you know deep down the person you've become isn't the real you. You may be feeling incomplete, directionless, confused, insecure, inauthentic, or unloved . . . even if your external appearance to others appears to indicate a successful life.

You so want to find that person who is your authentic self . . . who is confident, in control, peaceful, independent yet connected with others, loved and loving, secure, and flowing with life.

Despite your valiant efforts searching out there for the answer, and then taking action to improve your life, you still feel incomplete and inauthentic.

The elusive "I" has still not been found.

"I" IS NOT WHAT YOU THINK IT IS

Most people believe "I" is found in the sum total of their current appearance, thoughts, behaviors, and life circumstances. Who they are, they believe, is composed of how they look, their remembered past and imagined future, their resulting reactions to life, and how life is showing up for them.

We've been taught by our parents, peers, and schools that this is who we are. Then it's reinforced by society at large as we become adults. "I" is who we have become to this point in our life . . . and we accept it.

This manufactured self-concept feels so solid, so real, but it's not. It actually is what I call your small self, represented by "i" (small "i"). It is not authentic. It's a personality patched together over a lifetime from many external sources. For many people, their own input has been minimal. They have, unwittingly, participated in its construction unconsciously and automatically.

YOU'RE LOST IN A FOG

I'll never forget an experience I had coming back from college to my home on the Oregon Coast. I was driving on a winding country road. It was a dark night with low clouds. I came around a sweeping curve that dipped down into a small ravine. A bank of fog had settled into the ravine. As I

4

descended into this fogbank, everything disappeared. I could see absolutely nothing but the fog. It was an incredibly dangerous, unsettling experience. Fortunately, I quickly came out the other side of the fogbank without crashing.

You are lost in a fog of inauthenticity, floundering about in life, feeling disconnected and afraid. You can't seem to find your way out. You know this fog isn't you, but you don't know which direction to turn.

The "thick fogbank" you're living in acts as a veil that separates you from who you truly are and from the source of your true power. Until you're able to pierce through the veil of the fog, to get to the other side, you will not live an authentic life and realize your full potential.

"I" IS AT YOUR CENTER

The authentic "I" you're looking for exists within you at your center . . . at the core of who you truly are. It has always been and will remain there, waiting patiently for you to rediscover it. It's within you beyond the fog of your current existence. It has unlimited power that will transform your current history and circumstances.

Finding and experiencing "I" at your center will answer the age-old question, "Who am I?"

YOUR TRANSFORMATIONAL JOURNEY TO "I" . . . TO DISCOVER THE CORE OF WHO YOU REALLY ARE

Yet realization of "I" has been elusive for the vast majority of people.

Trying to find yourself from within the individual and

collective fog doesn't work. It reminds me of a great saying: "If you always do what you've always done, you'll always get what you've always got."

I know because this was my journey through life as well. I was trying to find answers to lead a better life in my own fog . . . trying to get answers from those influencers around me living in their own respective fog and quiet desperation.

Never Give Up! There is a way—I-Lignment—and reading this book is the beginning of the journey from living from your weak, inauthentic "i" to living from your powerful, authentic "I." The journey and destination are amazing!

Embedded in I-Lignment are many of the simple and powerful truths of life I mentioned earlier. There are two core truths that I want to mention up front. As you read each of these truths, you may completely understand and agree with them. You may also be skeptical. If you don't quite buy in, then keep yourself open to the possibility both are true. I believe by the end of the book you'll come to see them both as powerful core truths.

CORE TRUTH #1: "WE ARE ALL LOOKING FOR ONE THING IN LIFE . . . UNCONDITIONAL LOVE"

That's all we really want. Everything we do is because we want to feel and receive love without conditions. We want to fill the big, gaping void. Everything we do is either an expression of love or a cry for love. We want to love ourselves, we want to love others, and we want others to love us . . . unconditionally.

Most of us feel little or no unconditional love. We look for it out there in the world, in the very place where it's almost nonexistent. Conditional love exists, but unconditional love is scarce. All of us are looking for unconditional love from each other, but we are not finding it . . . nor are we offering it.

The irony is that it already exists in each one of us in unlimited quantities. We can't see it, though, because we're lost in the fog like everyone else . . . all separated from that true part of ourselves.

From the very core of who we are flows unconditional love. We no longer need to look for it "out there"; when we find it within ourselves, we ARE unconditional love. By practicing staying in connection with this authentic part of ourselves, we begin to radiate unconditional love to others indiscriminately. This is the crown jewel as you journey to and rediscover your true, authentic "I."

The saying "Love life and life will love you back" becomes more meaningful. When you find the unconditional love within, it flows out into the world in unlimited quantities and is reflected back to you as unconditional love.

When you discover this experientially, you'll know that it's true. As I mentioned, I had this profound experience myself and knew it, in that moment, as truth. As you go through your own transformation, you, too, will have this revelation.

The most important thing to do for your children is to teach them how to unconditionally love themselves and others. If this is all you teach your kids, they will have an incredibly strong foundation for a successful life. This has been the basis of my parenting for my boys from the time they were conceived to the present moment. I make sure they know I have unconditional love for them now and forever!

CORE TRUTH #2: "THE TRANSFORMATIONAL JOURNEY TO 'I' IS CRITICAL TO YOU AND THE WORLD . . . BECAUSE YOU'RE ALWAYS CREATING"

You're ALWAYS in the process of CREATING! Creating your life . . . and creating your world!

Every day, every minute, every second, you're creating your life and influencing the world around you by how you feel, think, and speak—and by the actions you take. You have no neutral emotions, thoughts, words, or actions . . . each one creates. But what are you creating and what is its source?

There are two sources of creating . . . and the source you pick determines your destiny.

For most people, their source of creating is their own and others' small self ("i"). This is a personal world, described earlier, that is incomplete, out of control, confused, fearful, disconnected, and lacking in unconditional love. It is filled with disjointed and inhibiting beliefs, judgments, and negative emotional charges . . . all brought forward from a dysfunctional past and projected into the future. This creates much suffering in our lives and in the lives of others.

I think you'll agree this isn't the type of life nor the world we want to continue to live in . . . it isn't sustainable.

The great news is that there's a second source of creating . . . from your true, authentic "I." And you have the freedom to pick which source you live from—"i" or "I." You can create from a source of unconditional love and peace, or from a source of fear, dysfunction, and uncertainty.

The type of world you create for yourself and for those around you . . . and beyond . . . depends on you, and it starts with you. The journey to transform the world is first an internal journey you must take yourself. Only then can you, by the way you show up in the world, begin to make a transformational difference.

It's imperative that you and all the rest of us take this journey and live life differently!

You're creating now! Let's see what type of life you've been creating . . .

CHAPTER TWO:
WHY? WHY IS MY LIFE LIKE THIS?

A LIFE CREATED FROM THE OUTSIDE-IN

You're probably asking yourself, "Why is my life like this and how the heck did I get here?" As a life coach, I hear this question all the time. People are perplexed why things have turned out the way they have; it's as if life has just happened to them out of their control.

You're at an important crossroad in your life. You have asked the question and are looking for answers.

Since I don't know you personally, I obviously can't discuss your specific situation. So, instead, I'll follow the life of a typical person I've coached:

Amber knows her life can be so much better than it is. She just turned forty-five, and as she goes through a tough time, she realizes she has fallen far short of her goals, both personally and professionally. She's confused because she thought she had been doing all that was expected of her. She's been spending a lot of time reflecting on her life to see if she can find answers to why life has turned out the way it has.

Amber had a typical childhood that had great moments but also tough times. Both her parents had rough childhoods. Her mom had been abused and ignored as a child, and her dad had a father who was a perfectionist and was extremely stern and controlling. Both her parents wanted to be much better parents for her and her siblings. Her parents, for the most part, tried to do the right thing, but they were not perfect.

Her parents were both working professionals with demanding jobs. They had a strong desire to make lots of money so they could provide a much better life for their kids. Despite talking about spending time with the kids, her mom and dad didn't have much quality time with any of them. They were always too busy. When Amber talked to them, even though they were talking to her, it seemed they were somewhere else in thought.

Despite their desire to parent better, Amber could see both her parents had continued to be impacted by their pasts. Her mom would fly off the handle at seemingly innocent remarks. She would say hurtful things to both Amber and her siblings. Her father, under the guise of wanting Amber to succeed in life, was stern and controlling.

Her parents had many conflicts with each other and argued often. As she entered her teen years, her parents had become increasingly distant and unloving to each other. Arguments increased in frequency until her parents got divorced when she was fifteen. Her dad left home to a city two hundred miles away, and she stayed with her mom, who became distant and self-absorbed. Amber felt abandoned and alone.

She couldn't wait to leave home and go to college. She made a commitment to herself to be different from her parents, to be an exceptional wife and mother and provider for her family. Her drive to be the ideal person was strong.

She picked a software-development degree because she thought it was the profession that would allow her to make lots of money and one that would make her parents, family, and friends proud. She focused on completing a four-year degree with top grades. She got input from family, friends, and mentors to determine what knowledge, skills, personality traits, and appearance would be expected of her in the working world . . . and she became that person.

Amber graduated from college, got a great job, met and married the man of her dreams, settled into a home, and had three children over the next eight years.

After their third child, the next seven years were great. Both she and her husband were doing all the "right things" as working professionals and parents. They were getting promotions and recognition at work, doing all that was expected of them. Their kids were thriving in school and with their friends. They had settled into a routine that seemed to work both for them and for everyone around them.

The relationship with her husband started changing and deteriorating over the next seven years. They both started feeling restless and unfulfilled. There was an ongoing feeling that something was missing. Emotions would appear out of the blue, triggered by each other, another person, or some event that would cause them to strongly react. They started to see faults in each other and became much more judgmental. Love was held back unless something was given or done by the other person. Her husband started drinking more frequently, especially after they had a fight. Amber would retreat and become passive aggressive in response to the verbal abuse she felt from him. Their home life became unbearable. To escape, Amber began spending a lot more time with her girlfriends, and her husband spent most of his time at work. Their kids felt the decreasing love and affection of their parents for each other. Both Amber and her husband retreated into their own little worlds and became less present for each other and their kids.

Amber, after forty-five years of building a life, now feels that whole time has been wasted. Her world is getting turned upside down. She's getting divorced after a twenty-one-year marriage. Her kids are getting ready to leave home for college. Older family and friends are starting to get sick and die. She's wondering who she really is after devoting herself to her husband and kids for the last twenty-one years. She has let her body and health take a back seat and is starting to feel the impact, especially with the stress she has right now. She feels stuck at her job now that she's about to be a single parent with greater responsibilities. She's starting to feel like life is getting short and is fearful about her future. She feels she has much less time left to create the life she really wants to live. She feels empty and sad. Something is missing at her very core.

She's desperate to find out what happened and where she should go from here.

Amber's situation is common. Perhaps some or the majority of it parallels your life. It's an example of how a life of inauthenticity is created, leading gradually to a moment where you intuitively realize it wasn't the life you wanted to create. This ultimate realization can be devastating. You've lost so many precious years of life to finally realize you need to change. Wouldn't it be great if you would have realized this at the very beginning of your life and made different, more aware choices? It's NEVER TOO LATE!

Before you can start making transformative changes, however, you need to understand how your life was constructed in the first place. You will see how haphazardly it was put together, why you have varying degrees of dysfunction, why your life isn't working for you, and why it's inauthentic. Most important, it'll give you even more incentive and commitment to create a life that is so much more powerful and authentic.

HOW DO YOU GET LOST IN THE FOG?

Remember, you're "always creating"—creating your life, creating your world. But what are you creating from? What is the *source* of this creative process right now?

The rest of this chapter will describe how our lives are formed and the impact this has on the quality of our ongoing life experience. As you read, take time to reflect how this applies to your life and current situation. Pay attention to your thoughts, emotions, and reactions that arise. Write them down. They'll be useful as you continue down your path of transformation.

———

There are four major stages in the process of creating a person: Emotional Development, Emotional-Mental Development, Mental-Physical Development, and Physical-Social Development. The impact of each stage impacts the next stage, and all are cumulative. These four stages create the core foundation and structure for a person's current life . . . their "inauthentic" personality . . . their "i" (small "i").

Let's explore these four stages.

EMOTIONAL DEVELOPMENT (Dominates between Conception and Eighteen Months)

When we're conceived, we're in the womb of our mother. We're not visible to others yet but are a living, growing human being. This is a time when it doesn't appear we're impacted by much, but, in reality, the emotional energy that surrounds us, especially from our mother, has a big impact on our emotional growth and well-being.

If we're fortunate, our mother is calm, peaceful, and loving during pregnancy. We dwell in this positive energy, and it becomes part of us. On the other hand, our mother may be agitated, angry, or depressed during pregnancy. We then dwell in this negative energy, and it becomes part of us. Fortunately, the nurturing side of a mother is naturally amplified during pregnancy, and the tendency is to be full of love and concern for the well-being of their baby.

We're typically born as a "little bundle of love." It is why people are so attracted to newborns. We can feel the unconditional love emanating from them. We love hugging and holding them. As parents, especially the mother, there is normally a special bond—a strong and deep loving connection forged during pregnancy.

After we're born, our emotions and behaviors are authentic and automatic. We're pure authenticity . . . loving, laughing, crying, cooing, pooping, peeing, and eating. The only thing that exists is the present moment.

"Like a freshwater stream flowing from a natural spring, so the emotional energy flows naturally from a newborn."

As a baby, we're intuitively looking for the same level of presence, unconditional love, and authenticity from others that we're giving to them, especially from our parents. Instead, many times our parents and others are distracted (not present) or are offering conditional love . . . sometimes no love at all. In fact, parents often are looking to their babies to give them unconditional love that they feel is lacking in their own lives. Lack of presence, unconditional love, and authenticity can create a feeling of emptiness we seek to fill. It begins a lifelong search for these emotions in an external world where they are extremely rare.

Our parents are separate from us, and we naturally begin to separate ourselves from them. This is the beginning of the creation of a separate, inauthentic self . . . the small "i." This separation creates many common and powerful emotions such as "feeling abandoned," "feeling unloved," and "feeling incomplete or not good enough."

Other people increasingly tell us how we should feel and

act through their reaction to our behavior, their facial or body expressions, their tone of voice, and their own emotional behavior. An example of this is when a parent gets frightened by something and reacts in strong fear. Their child sees this reaction to the event and becomes frightened, even though they had no prior experience with what was happening.

We begin to build an internal reservoir of both positive and negative emotional charges. Both the positive and negative emotions in this internal reservoir increasingly become what drives our individual behavior. Something outside of us triggers one of these emotional charges, and we automatically react.

So begins the process of shaping who we're supposed to emotionally be . . . from the outside-in.

Our individual fog begins to form . . .

EMOTIONAL-MENTAL DEVELOPMENT (Dominates between Eighteen Months and Six Years)

As we become more aware after eighteen months, we continue to absorb the emotional content of our parents and others around us. We become acutely aware of their emotional reactions and reflect them in our own life.

The development of us mentally also starts as we begin to communicate with our parents and an increasing number of other people. Others are now able to tell us what we should feel, think, say, and act when certain things happen. Even an experience that is seemingly only our own experience is interpreted by others for us. Once again they tell us how we should feel, think, say, and act as a result of "our" experience. We get this external input by being taught outright by others, by observing others, and by having experiences with others.

Our external emotional-mental programming has started. We are trained to take our direction from outside of us. Therefore, when we seek guidance, we once again look outside ourselves for the answers . . . how to feel, think, and act.

Since the input is increasingly coming from many sources, typically not coordinated, the input is disjointed, conflicted, and reflective of the dysfunctional life of the person providing the input. If we're unfortunate, on top of normal external input from others, we may experience traumas—accidents, parents' divorce, abandonment, or abuse.

This life-development phase, as well as the next, are critical because they lay the foundation for many of our core beliefs. Our life is being formed from the sum total of all these beliefs and associated emotional/verbal/physical reactive patterns. They're the beginning of forming our concept of who we are in this world and how to interact with others. The beliefs with the strongest emotional content have staying power and have the greatest influence on who we become. These strong beliefs also increasingly separate us from others.

Our individual fog becomes thicker and denser . . .

MENTAL-PHYSICAL DEVELOPMENT (Dominates between Seven and Thirteen Years)

Our lives now, in this phase, are focused more on mental development and how we relate to the world physically. As we enter school, being emotional is discouraged, while developing our minds is encouraged.

Our minds become of paramount importance. We're taught what to think and how to think . . . by others. We're given guidance and the hope that if we improve ourselves and gain greater knowledge and experience, then we'll be able to productively fit into society.

Emotional growth is stunted. However, since emotional awareness and growth is slowed or stopped with this new focus on the mind, the ability to resolve emotional dysfunction is slowed or stopped as well. Negative or inhibiting emotions that existed prior to this shift to mental-physical development are covered up by our growing thinking minds. Many of the unresolved, hidden childhood emotions and beliefs impact us the rest of our lives. These stifled emotions generate thousands of thoughts, many of which are quite immature. We may never progress emotionally beyond this point. The stifled emotions become part of who we are because we carry them forward rather than just experiencing them, resolving them, and letting them flow on by.

Our developing minds are like a dam on a river. The mental dam becomes wider and higher as we learn more and are told to stop being so emotional, slowing the natural flow of "emotional" water. These emotions begin to fill up the emotional reservoir behind the dam. The emotional reservoir becomes stagnant. The pressure on the dam begins to increase, especially if we have a lot of negative emotions. Our lives are dam'ed. This buildup continues until the pressure behind the dam is released, either incrementally, as in water pouring out through cracks in the dam, or as a major life event, as in a catastrophic failure of the dam, or as a conscious choice to get back to a natural emotional flow, as in the removal of the dam.

"Time" becomes important. Later in this phase, the concept of time starts to take on a greater role in our lives. We're taught that remembering "history" (both personal and societal) is important and is to be used as an ongoing foundation for our future. Time becomes a core part of everything we do. We now spend a lot of time thinking about the past as well as the future. The present moment is consumed resolving issues of the past. It's also taken up planning for a better future. The present becomes a stepping-stone to something better . . . later!

Our physical body "outlines" who we are. In addition to the focus on developing the mind, we and everyone around us begin to place a greater emphasis on our physical body as defining who we are . . . as well as how we relate to others. Our physical body "embodies" our emotional and mental development to this point. It encapsulates us and creates yet another layer of separation from others. We begin to see ourselves and others as separate and distinct physical entities with our own emotional and mental makeup. The people around us and society in general let us know how they perceive us, accept us or not, and how we fit into their world or not . . . based on appearance, behavior, and life circumstances. Since we have well learned by now to take our cues from external sources, we take others' opinions on how we look and behave seriously. Their opinion matters, and it's incorporated into how we see ourselves.

Our individual fog becomes even more thick and dense . . .

PHYSICAL-SOCIAL DEVELOPMENT (Dominates between Fourteen and Twenty-Five Years)

Now that we have created this separate, physical person, our personal development shifts to a focus on creating "social distinction and specialness"—a more defined and refined separation from others.

So begins the process of making up for perceived personal shortcomings that are fueled by internal limiting beliefs, such as "I'm not good enough," "I'm not loved," and "I've been abandoned," as well as the external expectations and judgments from others. These efforts by us are done to fit in, to be accepted, to be valued, and to connect in society in general as well as with specific people or groups of people.

The forces of society are also more than willing to help in the process of shaping who we are. These forces are endless: schools, news media, magazines, advertising, peer groups, social groups, employers, politicians, and social media, to name a very few.

How each "distinction and specialness" shows up for us depends on many factors and ranges from very empowering to very disempowering. It's important to understand, however, whether the "distinction and specialness" is empowering or disempowering, the source of their creation and evolution is mostly from outside us.

Authenticity took a back seat a long time ago.

The fog is now very thick and very dense . . . we're lost in it, and it's all we can see.

LIVING THE EFFECT . . . STUCK IN THE FOG

In our lives, our foundation, structure, and facade is now complete. This is who we've become . . . and this is who we think we are!

We are these patched-together lives that had input from many unrelated, uncoordinated, and, many times, dysfunctional sources. We've been unconsciously complicit in their construction . . . and are now their owner.

How our lives have been constructed reminds me of the odd Winchester Mystery House in San Jose, California.

The Winchester Mystery House was once owned by Sarah Winchester, the widow of William Winchester, the firearm magnate. After her husband's death, a Boston medium told her, while channeling her late husband, that she should travel west, find a property, and continuously build a home for herself and the spirits of those people killed by the Winchester rifles. Mrs. Winchester thought her family and wealth were haunted by ghosts and, by following the advice of the medium and building the house, she could appease these spirits.

She began construction of the house around the clock with no overall master plan. Carpenters added on to the building, uninterrupted, in a haphazard manner for thirty-six years, resulting in a seven-story, 161-room, two-basement, and forty-seven-fireplace mansion that contains many strange features, including doors and stairs that go nowhere, windows looking into other rooms in the house, and stairs with different-size risers.

Despite how haphazardly our lives have been constructed, it's who we identify as our "i" (small "i") . . . we are our own Winchester Mystery House. As we move forward in life, we may change our facade—in other words, give our life a facelift—but the underlying foundation and structure usually remains the same.

We constructed ourselves to be who others wanted us to be and to feel accepted and safe in the world. Our lives are set and solidified as others show agreement with who we think we've become. And we're stuck with this life . . . so we think.

With our acceptance, it becomes the basis for the rest of our life. We live the same life over and over and over, reacting to the makeup of our life created from the outside-in. This is why life feels routine, boring, confusing, and insincere.

This is our "source of life" now. Everything we do is directly influenced by this hodgepodge self we have created or which has been created for us up to now. Is it any wonder we ask the question, "Who am I?"

So how does all this impact how we show up in life?

––––

We're inauthentic, sourcing our life from . . . Out There!

As we build this life from the outside-in, we gradually lose touch with our true self that is free flowing and authentic. It's getting buried by the input from others. We mimic the inauthenticity of the people around us. We absorb and accept many of their beliefs and the intrinsic emotion of each belief . . . both empowering and disempowering. We begin to build the "stories" of our life . . . a string of interconnected beliefs based mostly on external input or interpretation. All these beliefs and stories, derived from the input of others, form our view of the world around us . . . as well as how we perceive ourselves. We are "formed" . . . molded . . . into something separate from our authentic self.

The makeup of this inauthentic self is, then, reflected in how we talk about ourselves . . . "i" am _____ (small "i"). It's the verbal articulation of how we feel and think inside . . . our beliefs. How we articulate ourselves in each area of our lives falls somewhere between empowering and disempowering.

Disempowering	Empowering
"i" am stupid	"i" am intelligent
"i" am weak	"i" am strong
"i" am not good enough	"i" am highly capable
"i" am alone	"i" am popular
"i" am fat	"i" am in perfect shape
"i" am abandoned	"i" am part of the family
"i" am unloved	"i" am loved
"i" am a victim	"i" am powerful
"i" am shy	"i" am outgoing
"i" am fearful	"i" am brave
"i" am a grunt	"i" am a highly capable warehouse stocker

We identify with our *"i" am*s . . . and the underlying beliefs and stories of our life. They become embedded into our conscious and subconscious. Their truth is mostly not questioned, and we accept them as "me" . . . our inauthentic self. Life beyond our formative years (birth to twenty-five years) continues to expand on this inauthentic base.

Trying to create an authentic self by discovering and building it from out there is fruitless and exasperating. It isn't out there. Out there is only copying, trying to live someone else's life, a life that is not our own. There's no continuity and cohesiveness in living this type of life, because it changes constantly and is influenced daily by all those around us. It's full of uncertainty and fear. If those around us don't support who we are and the actions we take, who we are ceases to be valid. We grasp for their support and validation, and if we don't receive it, we look to how we can change to once again gain their acceptance and to reestablish our outside-in identity. The inauthentic self is our fragile identity . . . easily shattered.

We identify with power . . . Out There!

As we develop, we take cues from our environment for how we should live our lives—cues from our family, friends, bosses, peers, social groups, doctors, politicians, and even from strangers as they walk past us on the street. This is amplified when we believe we need someone else to complete us . . . that we're not good enough by ourselves . . . resulting in codependence.

Society supports this approach for all sorts of reasons and in all sorts of ways. We hear things like, "It's always been done this way," "Listen to the experts, they know more than you," "Follow your bosses' orders without question and you won't get in trouble," "Don't question authority," "Follow the rules without question," "You're a victim, and only we can help you."

Since the source of input for our lives has been outside of us, we believe the source of power lies outside of ourselves as well. We begin to look for ways to plug into that external power. As we look for our power increasingly from others, we lose the connection with our own internal power. This creates a neediness of others and a desire to control others.

Getting guidance and our power for our lives entirely outside of ourselves creates a life of quiet desperation, with the outside forces that we're pursuing constantly buffeting us around and pulling us in different, often conflicting directions. These outside forces lock us into a way of life that doesn't feel real and is out of our control.

We've given our power away! People who understand this can manipulate and control us.

We flow with life . . . Out There!

Since we've built our lives from the input and power of others out there, we attempt to get into the flow of life outside of ourselves. We see this outside flow as something we need to get into with others to be successful.

We've allowed ourselves to be influenced from the out-side-in . . . and then embedded ourselves in the flow of the outside world around us. We learn to act from external cues or requests of others rather than be driven from our own internal motivation. We end up getting involved in, attaching to, and reacting to so many things that are unimportant to us; we become buried in the demands and distractions of the outer world.

We, therefore, become reactive to life. Our life is not our own. We work hard to figure out how we can best fit into this outer flow rather than creating our own life from within. We can become so enmeshed in our outer life that our inner life becomes almost nonexistent. We become lost to ourselves . . . only living the way the world wants us to live.

We perceive that what's happening to us is caused by something . . . Out There!

Most of us are aware of the concept of cause and effect. We

can see it all the time in the world around us. But most of us have a huge personal flaw. We can't see the principle of cause and effect as it applies to us and our behavior. Since we've created our life outside-in, we believe the cause is out there. This is compounded by the fact that many of our emotional issues are buried in our subconscious, so we can't even begin to make the connection between the cause and the effect. The world chaotically happens and then it affects us. We believe everything happening in our lives is the fault of something out there in the world . . . a person or an event.

When we project our anger and blame outward and attack the world, the world reflects this attack back. What we see is a world filled with "enemies" ready to strike at us. Thus, we build up defenses all around ourselves to protect against these perceived threats. This is our reality . . . a vicious cycle of attack, building defenses, perceiving being attacked, continuing to strengthen defenses, and counterattack. That is, until we understand how we can see the world differently and change our thinking.

We do something (thinking, verbal, or action) that creates an immediate effect on the world around us, but we don't see it immediately. We may see the effect later, but it shows up as a reflection back to us from the world around us. We therefore think the cause is out there and, therefore, the change that needs to take place is out there as well.

Because of this, when we feel a strong internal emotional reaction, we believe the cause was from the thing out there that triggered the emotion. What we're not seeing is the underlying initial cause of that emotion, which may have happened years before, perhaps in our childhood. The current event was just a trigger of an emotion or belief buried inside of us.

By assigning blame in the outside world, we have disempowered ourselves. Now there is no way for us to alter our life experience because someone or something out there needs to change first. This is the beginning of learning how to be a victim. To clarify, being victimized is real and is a tragic event. *Being a victim* is a way of life and is not real . . . it's just a disempowering belief.

Right now, our emotions, thoughts, words, and actions are being created out of our inauthentic life . . . a fog filled with emotional and mental dysfunction, conflict, and confusion caused by past events we've carried forward into the present. As long as we have emotional turmoil within, and don't understand the internal cause of those emotions, we'll continue to resort to many dramas, accusations, and blame directed at the outside world.

We live on autopilot, reacting to people and events . . . Out There!

As we get triggered more and more by our internal emotions and underlying beliefs, the reactions become habits; therefore, the reactions become automatic. In addition, many of the strongest negative emotionally charged beliefs are buried in our subconscious. We don't even know they exist. They reside in our subconscious because they become too painful to process in our conscious life. When we get triggered, we don't even know why we're reacting the way we are . . . and neither does anyone else.

As we add an increasing number of emotionally charged beliefs to our lives with predetermined responses, our life increasingly shifts to a life on autopilot. This thing happens in life, and we automatically react in a predictable way. We think we're consciously responding but, in reality, we're reacting based on an emotionally charged belief from the past.

We're now, to a great extent, on autopilot the majority of the time . . . not living in the present moment but, rather, reacting from the past. We're no longer in charge of our lives . . . our past outside-in programming is. We're controlled by an internal, unconscious program guiding our every movement.

We're living the past . . . over and over and over. We're no longer living life; our manufactured life is living us.

We attempt to change "ourselves" . . . Out There!

As mentioned earlier, we believe who we are is the combination of our appearance, behaviors, and life circumstances . . . and others agree with us. Because we're feeling empty, incomplete, and lack in our lives, we spend a great deal of time, money, and energy doing things to change who we think we are. We spend a great part of our lives focused on changing our appearance, behaviors, and life circumstances. Since we became disconnected from our own real emotional growth a long time ago, the changes we seek are primarily physical and mental.

Unfortunately, since we've been taught to take cues outside of ourselves to determine what's best, we look to others outside of ourselves to determine what changes to make. We're set up to be controlled by others . . . intentionally or unintentionally. The outside-input we're receiving on a daily basis on what changes to make to be more successful in life is endless, conflicting, and confusing, since the world around us is constantly changing and the suggested changes come from many uncoordinated sources. This leads to a lifetime pursuit of doing things to improve ourselves . . . led by others.

In reality, our appearance, behaviors, and life circumstances are, to a great extent, the effect of internal causes (emotions, beliefs, and stories) based on the type of life we've constructed to date. It's these internal causes that need to be adjusted to transform our lives.

However, we think the cause and solution are out there somewhere, so that's where we seek the change. We make demands for change and set up goals to accomplish the change . . . out there with others. Some of the demands/goals are documented, while others are subtle. As we encounter more and more situations, we see the demands and goals conflict with one another. We accomplish change in one part of our world, only to have it conflict with another. There is no overall unified outcome in mind.

We end up pursuing these changes with little true transformation in our lives. The real internal cause has not yet been altered.

We desperately seek unconditional love . . . Out There!

One of the biggest changes we desire is to find more love in our lives. Unconditional love is all we have ever wanted, and is the only thing we want in life, whether we are conscious of it or not. This is a fundamental truth.

We had it when we were born but, unless we were lucky, it may not have been reciprocated by others when we were children. We were given conditional love or no love at all. An unconditional love "void" was created. Therefore, it set us off on a lifelong quest to find it somewhere out there in the world . . . a world where unconditional love is rare.

But if we're like so many others who have been searching for years and never finding unconditional love, we may not believe unconditional love even exists. We've given up and have replaced it with an acceptance of conditional love or substituted it with forms of imitation love . . . to fill the emptiness we feel inside.

Conditional love creates happiness but is not consistent and often goes away when the "condition" for that love is not given by us. Conditional love creates feelings of being controlled, manipulated, needing to please, or being on edge. We know it has the possibility of going away, so if we want that love to continue, we need to always put in a lot of thought and effort to make sure we're measuring up to the other person's expectations.

Imitation love, as a poor substitute for unconditional love, creates a fragile happiness. It takes on thousands of forms in four main categories: Praise, Pleasure, Safety, and Power.

Praise: We feel "loved" when people say things like "You're beautiful," "You're so smart," "You're incredibly talented," "You have accomplished so much," and "You're unbelievably organized." Because of this, we're constantly seeking approval and validation from others.

Pleasure: We seek things that give us an emotional or physical rush, especially when given to us by another person—having sex, traveling, dining out, going to parties, shopping, gambling, drinking alcohol, and using drugs, among thousands of other pleasure-producing activities.

Safety: We seek and stay in relationships that make us feel safe—physically, emotionally, and financially. We're in the relationship because it feels familiar, comfortable, and predictable.

Power: We feel more powerful by being with certain people; they transfer power to us when we are in their presence. We may also use power over others as a substitute for love, especially if they willingly give us control over them.

We expend a tremendous amount of effort and time pursuing all the forms of imitation love, but the result is always the same: a short burst of pleasure followed by feelings of emptiness, nothing that adds long-term happiness to our lives, and certainly no unconditional love.

We forgot how to unconditionally love other people and ourselves a long time ago. Now conditional and imitation love are all we know. We'll do anything to get them so we can have at least some level of happiness in our lives. And we do, but it always leads back to a feeling of aloneness and emptiness.

We "want" things . . . Out There!

The lack of love and emptiness we feel inside leads to a belief we are missing something in our lives. We feel incomplete. We have feelings of lack. We need something, anything, to make ourselves whole. This leads to many "wantings" to fill that void. And, of course, we then pursue these wantings outside of ourselves, because we've been taught that anything of value to us exists out there somewhere.

- Wanting unconditional love
- Wanting presence
- Wanting completeness
- Wanting control
- Wanting approval
- Wanting security
- Wanting to feel separate, special, and attractive
- Wanting to be supported
- Wanting change
- Wanting acceptance
- Wanting peace
- Wanting happiness
- Wanting companionship
- Wanting money
- Wanting possessions

If we examine all aspects of our lives honestly, we'll find the list of wants is extensive. We expend a tremendous amount of time and energy pursuing all these wants. But when we get what we want, it never fills the emptiness and aloneness we feel within. Maybe for a short time, but certainly not long term.

This leads to a life of wanting, wanting, wanting . . . of endless doing to fulfill the wants . . . of sometimes getting what we want but never feeling satisfied and happy in the long run. A life of limitation, scarcity, and fear . . . of always looking to the future for fulfillment and happiness.

We cope with life . . . Out There!

Despite all our efforts to change our lives—to find

unconditional love and a sense of peace, to fill the void of emptiness, to satisfy our wants, and to eliminate the feelings of discomfort, uncertainty, confusion, and fear—nothing of significance has changed. We're still dealing with drama, commotion, and issues in our life. The underlying causes are still there, and so are the effects we experience.

It's a natural human instinct to move toward pleasure and away from pain. We've tried everything to move toward pleasure, but those efforts have not removed the pain and discomfort generated by the underlying causes. So now, instead, we focus our attention on moving away from the pain and discomfort. And we'll do just about anything to get away from it.

If you've ever gone camping at a campground, you've inevitably had the experience of going to an outdoor, open-pit toilet that hasn't been cleaned for a while . . . the awful smell is overpowering. The only thing that consumes your attention in the moment is the smell. You can't think of anything but how to get away from it. This is what happens when you're buried in the mess of your life. You so desperately want to escape it and find "fresh air." Not knowing how to clean out the tank, you devise many ways to escape from the smell or to cover it up.

We, therefore, begin coping with life as it is, not by trying to change the underlying cause, but by dealing with the ongoing effects of it in our lives and the pain it creates. We learn coping techniques through observation of others or by being taught by others. We may have used one or more of these primary ways of coping.

Accept: If we can't change the internal discomfort that we feel or the external reflection of that discomfort, we may decide to accept it as part of our life experience. We're still getting impacted by it, perhaps severely, but we've decided not to do anything about it.

Ignore: We may also pretend like it doesn't exist. It's like an ostrich sticking its head in the sand. We're still getting impacted by it, but we're pretending we're not.

Reject: We may also not accept its validity in our lives. It still exists and is impacting us, but we just reject the fact that it is or that its impact is all that important.

Escape: Running away from the problem is another way to deal with the discomfort, such as by moving to another city or quitting a job. We're leaving the problem behind . . . so we think.

Project: This mode of coping is common, especially in our society, which seems to honor being a victim. Since we can't see the cause within ourselves, it feels good to assign the blame to someone or something else out there. We attack the outside perceived cause and project our anger and judgment on them. It relieves the internal pressure in the moment. However, it creates a new set of problems in our lives since the real cause is not what we have just set our sights on, but rather is one that still exists within us.

Suppress: When negative events and emotions occur that are too much for us to handle, we suppress them into our subconscious. This is not done by choice. Because they're submerged below our consciousness, we don't have to see them or deal with them anymore, which reduces the immediate discomfort.

There they lie, however, beyond our awareness, waiting to be triggered by outside people and events, or our own internal dialog. The link between the emotion and the original cause (person or event) has been hidden, so when that emotion is triggered in the present, the current person/event gets the full brunt of the responsibility for making us feel that way. We know this is happening when the reaction is so much more powerful than what is warranted for the current situation. Many times, the person that is the target of the powerful reaction is baffled and clueless as to why they're being blamed in such a harsh way.

Cover up: When we cover up, we essentially put a blanket over our emotional issues to sedate them, so we don't have to see and feel them anymore. Society has invented an infinite number of ways to do this: drinking alcohol, using drugs, gambling, overworking, shopping, overeating, engaging in too much screen time, and becoming obsessively involved with our kids and spouse, to name a few.

Even though all these coping mechanisms may seem to work for us in the short term, the underlying issue that triggered us to cope in the first place is still there. If not resolved, the underlying cause of any discomfort in our life will inevitably rise once again to the surface and demand our attention. It will continue to do this over and over until we finally resolve it. Because coping isn't serving us well, our life can become an emotional ticking time bomb, waiting to explode.

Addictions. One way this time bomb shows up is through addictions. We may have been using various ways to cover up the discomfort, including alcohol, drugs, gambling, shopping, and sex, to name a few. As we continue to use these cover-ups as a necessary way to sedate and control the internal discomfort, they turn into habits, which lead to addictions empowered by the continuing presence of the underlying cause. This is significantly amplified if we have a genetic predisposition to any of the addictions.

Afflictions. A second way the time bomb is expressed is through afflictions such as allergies, minor illnesses, major illnesses, and death. This is the body's way of reacting to the unresolved, pent-up emotional issues. The "dis-ease"—which implies the lack of ease in your internal life—contributes to many health issues.

Major Life Events. A third way the time bomb is expressed is through major life events, including divorce and suicide. Our underlying emotions continue to build up through coping until the pressure becomes too much and it explodes all at once, resulting in a major change in our life. The emotional release, based on the current situation and solution, is swift and provides immediate relief from the pressure . . . but no real resolution.

Beneath all our frantic coping, and the resulting addictions, afflictions, and major life events, still lies the discomfort or pain that is driving all the external activities. Despite all our efforts, we still don't feel good. Until resolved, the underlying issues will continue to exist and will once again build up emotional pressure until they burst to the surface of our lives to get our attention.

We're stuck in the inauthentic "canyon" of life ... Out There!

The development of our life has led us to this point in time. It's an inauthentic life created from the outside-in.

TO RECAP ...

- We are inauthentic by virtue of sourcing the development of ourselves from others.
- We identify with and seek power outside of ourselves and, as we do, have lost connection with our own internal power.
- We flow with life outside of ourselves ... a flow that is predominantly driven by others and in alignment with time, especially the remembered past and a projected future. The present moment is used as a stepping-stone and isn't lived well.
- Since we source our lives and power from out there, we also perceive that the cause of things (good or bad) happening to us and for us are from out there as well.
- If we feel a need to change or improve ourselves due to feeling incomplete, inadequate, or "not good enough," we seek guidance for how to do so from the outside.
- We feel that unconditional love is lacking or nonexistent in our lives, so we seek it from other people.

If we can't find it, we look for other ways to replace it with either conditional love or imitation love.

- We have ended up with a long list of "wantings" to fill the emptiness and inadequacy we feel inside . . . and we are looking outside in the world to satisfy those wantings.
- We have developed multiple ways of coping with difficult aspects of the life we've created.

Once manufactured, our lives are supported and reinforced by all those around us, especially those who personally benefit from the person we've become. They want us to stay this way ad infinitum. It works for them . . . even if it's not working for us.

The Grand Canyon is a great metaphor for the life we're living. The Colorado River has carved the Grand Canyon over time, creating a clearly defined path on its journey. The tall walls of the canyon, etched with a long history, allow little leeway to the flow of the river. The river is trapped and held hostage by the canyon—it has no choice but to go one way. On its journey, the river has lengths of calm waters followed by incredibly turbulent rapids through fields of boulders and powerful eddies.

We allow others to create the "walls of our canyon" as well as the haphazard design and construction of our rickety "life" raft . . . all based on their own narrow and limited knowledge and perspective. They then help launch us into the flow of time. At first the canyon walls of our lives (composed of beliefs, emotions, and stories) were not too high, but as we continued down our life journey, the walls got higher and higher. Our past (upstream) became clearly defined and it, along with the momentum of our river of life with others, had a major influence on defining our future (downstream). Our experience, at any time, became limited by our canyon walls and the conditions of the river of life at that time.

Now our current moment is lived in anxiety of what might lie ahead downstream and the possibility of more rapids of life. If our "life" raft is not well designed, as we go through the rapids of life, our raft might start to fall apart and require us to patch it together in the hope we can make it to the other side of the canyon alive and in one piece. If we try to change directions during our life (rafting trip), the sheer height of the canyon walls of life that surround us make it difficult to escape and, in most cases, forces us to continue down the path of life defined by others as well as our own history.

We are trapped in our own Grand Canyon, with only one direction to go. Our past becomes a powerful predictor of our future.

————

COLLECTIVELY WE'RE LOST IN THE FOG

We're all lost in this fog together. Everyone is struggling and confused in their own way with their own unique life history and current life circumstances. As we interact with others, our patched-together, dysfunctional life is bumping up against their patched-together, dysfunctional lives . . . we get entangled with one another. At the same time, we all are asking the question "Who am I?" individually and "Who are we?" collectively. The world reflects this shared confusion. Is it any wonder the world feels a bit conflicted and chaotic, knowing now how our lives have been created?

We also know instinctively there's a better way of living, but we just don't know how to get there. It's like we're lost in a winter blizzard whiteout, unable to see our hands in front of our faces, knowing that our warm, comfortable home is close, but not knowing how to get there.

What now?

CHAPTER THREE:
THE MOMENT OF REALIZATION

MOST OF US have had moments when we realize something needs to change significantly in our life. We can no longer accept the status quo. Life just isn't working anymore. We no longer want to have that empty, dissatisfied feeling inside or what feels like a completely dysfunctional life. The future isn't exciting . . . or it's downright bleak. We're sick and tired of living this way!

My turning point was in my latter twenties, with the discovery of "how" to transform my life twenty-five years later!

IS THIS YOUR TURNING POINT?
Perhaps this is your moment . . . and is the reason you're reading this book. You've come to a pivotal point in your

life, where your current life is no longer acceptable. You're looking for a major change to a much better life. You realize you've been repeating life over and over, year after year. You NOW want to start living an exciting, authentic life. You're looking for freedom, personal freedom, to live the life of your dreams.

This deep desire is captured in the poem by Maya Angelou . . .

> *"But a bird that stalks down his narrow cage*
> *Can seldom see through his bars of rage*
> *His wings are clipped, and his feet are tied*
> *The caged bird sings with a fearful trill*
> *And his tune is heard on the distant hill for*
> *The caged bird sings of freedom."*

This is an incredibly powerful moment for you. This is the time to seize the opportunity to transform your life. Commit to doing whatever you need to do to make it happen! Commit to your personal freedom.

When most people reach this point, however, they don't know where to turn. They don't know how to take the first step toward "real" transformation.

You're lucky . . . read on.

CHAPTER FOUR:
FINDING YOUR PATH TO TRANSFORMATION

WHEN I STARTED searching in my early thirties for a way to transform my life, I couldn't find an approach that made sense to me and worked. There were so many options in the field of self-improvement.

Here is a list of a few that were being offered . . . Biofeedback, yoga, affirmations, visualization, meditation, antidepressants, chakras balancing, tapping, reflexology, acupuncture, chiropractic, psychic readings, Jazzercise, gestalt therapy, naturopathic medicine, kinesiology, hormone shots, vegetarianism, astral projections, organic eating, acupressure, shiatsu, isolation chambers, tarot card readings, psychic readings, fasting, health spas, travel to spiritual retreats, isolation, tantric sex, celibacy, herbal medicine, neurolinguistic programming, psychology, healing with crystals and light, chanting mantras, Rolfing, drumming, aerobics, colonics, motivational speakers, mentoring, macrobiotics, feng shui, special diets, swimming in a sacred body of water, plunging into ice-cold water, exploring past lives, finding a spiritual guide, changing your thoughts, subliminal programming, music therapy, sound therapy, wearing copper jewelry, therapeutic shoes, psychedelics . . . the list is endless.

Despite all my searching and trying different programs and workshops, most of them seemed to fall short. Some were effective in parts of my life but not in others. Some were effective but way too complex or took too much time to use day-to-day. Some made me feel good in the moment but were not effective long term. Some missed the mark completely. Some were downright scams.

So began my journey to create a transformative approach that I could apply to my life as well as share with others. It has taken me many years of self-reflection and self-discovery; attending workshops and retreats; researching and reading; realizing simple, powerful truths of life; and discovering simple yet powerful techniques.

So evolved the personal transformation process of . . .

I-Lignment.

Taking this journey of I-Lignment can be visualized once again through the metaphor of the Grand Canyon.

One day, during a long rafting trip through the Grand Canyon, you're having increasingly strong feelings of being trapped and out of control. Suddenly, you come across an abandoned hot-air balloon on one of the shores. This is your opportunity to escape and have a new experience in life. You climb into the basket, turn on the burners, and release the tie-down lines. The basket begins to rise. You climb higher and higher between the mile-high walls of the canyon. As you do, it becomes clear how you've been trapped and were destined down only one path defined by the canyon walls and flow of the river. As you climb even higher, you realize there is so much more to life than what you believed possible down there. There's an expansive landscape in all directions, with vistas, plateaus, rivers, wildlife, and people of all kinds to interact with everywhere. Your life has been instantaneously expanded to an unlimited number of possibilities for life experiences and adventures.

I-Lignment is your hot-air balloon! This is your opportunity to create an amazing life with unlimited possibility!

TRUST THE I-LIGNMENT PROCESS OF TRANSFORMATION . . . AND DO IT AS IF YOUR LIFE DEPENDS ON IT . . . BECAUSE IT DOES!

Trust the process of the book. It has been structured to facilitate both your new perspective and your journey to your authentic "I" . . . and then to create a powerful life from there. Trust the process even when you may feel confused or uncertain. Once you reach the end of the book, you'll have a new perspective and will be moving down the path of powerful personal transformation.

If you trust and apply I-Lignment, you will be . . .

CHAPTER FIVE:
LIVING LIFE POWERFULLY... FROM THE INSIDE-OUT

EVERYONE HAS GREATNESS WITHIN THEM ... COVERED UP BY LIFE!

You may be thinking, "No way. My life is so messed up. I feel so confused. I've tried in the past to change but only failed." We've all been there. But trust me, the incredible life you seek lies within . . . past the static of your current life. Greatness is already inside you, waiting to be uncovered, discovered, and then lived.

Once you find it, an incredibly bright light will shine through you out into the world. A light that is full of unconditional love and peace. One of authenticity and true connection. One of purpose and passion. One of contribution and being of service to others. One of abundance . . . for everyone.

You not only realize your own inner greatness, but you also see the true infinite beauty of the world around you that was formerly hidden by the fog of life. You see the connectedness of all living things. Being inspired becomes natural to you.

You also see the incredible possibilities to live whatever life you want to live in this world. You truly have discovered and are living your Greatest Life, a life of Inner Purpose, empowered creativity, and individual freedom.

EMPOWERED . . . SOURCING LIFE FROM THE INSIDE-OUT

Your Greatest Life is here . . . right now! You don't have to go anywhere to discover this life or wait until sometime in the future to realize it. You need to stay where you are and go within yourself.

You realize your Greatest Life by taking this inward journey to shift from a life created from the outside-in to a life created from the inside-out. An outside-in life is disempowering; it imprisons you by your past and allows you to be controlled by others. An inside-out life is incredibly empowering; it opens you to all possibilities, gives you maximum freedom, and allows you to create the life of your dreams.

Remember, you're always creating your life. Do you want to create your life from a source out there? Or would you rather create your life authentically from within you? How you ultimately experience your life depends on the choice of your creative source!

A Life Created and Lived "Outside-In" or "Inside-Out" . . . Your Choice! Choose "Inside-Out"!

When you do and are flowing inside-out from this new Source of Life, you show up dramatically different in the world . . .

- You feel authentic and real.
- You feel whole.
- Your newfound freedom is real . . . with unlimited possibilities.
- Your life is full of unconditional love . . . independent of anyone else.
- You experience waves of love coming from deep inside you.
- You have a deep sense of peace . . . no matter the circumstances outside of you.
- You live life powerfully . . . in each present moment.
- You have a whole new way of "being."
- You have found the feelings you want in your life are the feelings inherently felt at your core . . . your authentic "I."
- You experience an inner joy that is independent of anything outside of you.
- You have a newfound passion for life.
- You're less impacted by the flow of life outside of you.
- Your mind is clear and able to make quicker, better decisions.

- You're less reactive to the world around you; rather, you respond based on right actions.
- You now know you can handle whatever life throws your way.
- You look at the major events in your life differently.
- Many of the "wants" in your life have vanished.
- You're simplifying your life.
- You have more natural abundance in all parts of your life.
- Your life feels more effortless and enjoyable.
- Your relationships are deeper and more authentic.
- Your experience of "falling in love" with someone is now powerful and unconditional.
- You have become more accepting of others . . . as they are.
- You allow unlimited possibilities for others . . . beyond your own self-interests.
- You express many acts of kindness in your daily life.
- Your life is spacious and light.
- Your well-being becomes a natural state . . . not something you need to work at.
- Your inner discomfort or pain that drove your compulsive behavior is gone.
- You enjoy peace and quiet.
- Your energy increases dramatically.
- You have a deep sense of power you've never felt before.
- You have a personal connection with your Inner Power.
- You trust and follow your Inner Guidance.
- You don't need approval from others.

- You feel empowered . . . you're no longer a victim of life.
- You're committed to your purpose . . . something much greater than just yourself.
- Your creativity has been empowered.
- Your life is created . . . inside-out.
- You look at what might go right in life . . . as opposed to what might go wrong.
- Your life becomes more about contribution, adventure, experiences, and people . . . rather than the accumulation of stuff.
- Life becomes your playground.
- You feel "connected" with life.
- You feel a oneness . . . with all life.
- You naturally want to create a better world.

NOTE: Each one of the above will be discussed in more detail in Chapter Ten: "The Transformed You."

Now let's explore how this type of life is possible . . .

PART TWO:
TRANSFORMING YOUR LIFE

CHAPTER SIX:
I-LIGNMENT

NOW BEGINS THE exciting part! You're going to learn a new, powerful approach to transform your life. You're taking your first real steps down a path that will lead to your Greatest Life!

Real personal transformation isn't a process of doing something to improve the current you; it's a process of undoing and allowing the real you to emerge. I-Lignment is a journey inward, past your current outside-in life, to rediscover who you are authentically and then create your new, powerful life inside-out. Everything you've been looking for is waiting inside of you. You'll prove this to yourself by going through the process. It's a process that allows you to tap into and then live from your source of Inner Power and unlimited possibilities. It reverses your way of living . . . from "life living you" to "you living life." It will be the greatest journey you'll ever take.

I-Lignment is like metamorphosis, the process where a slinking caterpillar transforms into a beautiful, free butterfly. When it's time for the caterpillar to transform, it creates a cocoon around itself and allows its cells to begin to rearrange into something much grander than its current self. I-Lignment is the cocoon you're about to crawl inside to begin your own transformation.

SIMPLE YET POWERFUL TRANSFORMATIONAL PROCESS

I-Lignment is a simple, holistic, and deliberately guided process. You'll be brought into it first through reading the book, then by having a personal, powerful experience by going through the actual I-Lignment process in Part Five, and finally through living a life transformed by it.

The approach is natural and designed to be used in daily life . . . no matter your current circumstances. Since it integrates into your daily life and is therefore sustainable, it naturally transitions into being a powerful way of living life.

These main components of I-Lignment will be discussed in the following chapters.

Chapter Seven: The I-Model . . . a New Perspective for Personal Transformation. A new model for understanding life that is used as a guide for navigating the I-Lignment process.

Chapter Eight: Journey to the "I"ntersection. The inward journey past the inauthenticity of your current life to the powerful "I"ntersection of your life . . . your authentic "I."

Chapter Nine: Living Your Greatest Life . . . from "I." A process of creating your Greatest Life from the inside-out.

As you journey down the path of I-Lignment, you'll also transition through the Four Shifts of Personal Transformation, which are critical for any real change in your life: a Shift of Perspective, a Shift of Source, a Shift of Intention, and a Shift of Attention. The quality of your life experience is dependent on all four. You'll get the Shift of Perspective by reading the I-Lignment book first, and then you'll experience the Shift of Source, the Shift of Intention, and the Shift of Attention by going through the actual I-Lignment process.

THE JOURNEY IS YOUR OWN

This is how you get your authentic life, personal power, and freedom back . . . through I-Lignment!

And the only place this true transformation can begin is in the present moment. You can start I-Lignment right where you are . . . now. Do this without reservation or detour. A new beginning happens in an instant . . . by making a committed decision to change ourselves and to transform our lives into something much different and much better. One committed decision is all it takes to initiate the change and then begin the journey one moment at a time.

But it takes a real commitment and dedicated personal responsibility to stick with it. Your transformation is an inner personal journey. It depends on you and can only be done by you. Others can guide you, but no one can do it for you. The great news is that it can be done by only you without anyone's interference or help; there's no one who can stop you!

I-Lignment has, therefore, been designed specifically so you're empowered to do it on your own. Trust in the process. It has the power to transform your life if you take it seriously. Remember, you're in charge and, with I-Lignment, are empowered. Have faith your transformation will occur . . . and it will.

YOUR TRANSFORMATION JOURNEY

"Your Transformation Journey" is Part Five of the book. It's your guide (process and tools) for your own personal transformation. It's important you read the rest of the book before beginning the I-Lignment process. As I mentioned, one of the Four Shifts of Transformation is the Shift of Perspective. The remainder of the book will empower you with a new and powerful perspective that is necessary for the I-Lignment process to be effective in your life.

Let's begin . . .

CHAPTER SEVEN:
THE I-MODEL

A NEW LIFE MODEL FOR PERSONAL TRANSFORMATION

*"To change something, build a new model that
makes the existing model obsolete."*
—BUCKMINSTER FULLER

Personal development is complex and confusing, but it's increasingly so if you're trying multiple approaches that were created with different philosophies, language, and ways of applying them to your life. Since many personal development approaches apply to only one part of your life with no clear path to overall transformation, you're forced to use several to create your own holistic system of personal development; you're left to make sense of them and piece them together the best you can. Many don't even get to the cause of the issues in your life. Most of the time they leave you with a personal development system that looks very much like your life: disjointed, confusing, not very effective, and dependent on others for your transformation.

YOU'RE LOST . . . WITH THE WRONG MAP!

Without a correct perspective that models how your life has been created to date and how you can transition out of it to a better life, you most likely will remain stuck and unsure how to move your life forward.

Imagine you are on a trip to New York City. As you approach the city at night, you reach into your glove box filled with maps and pull out the one for New York . . . or so you think. You start to navigate the crisscrossing array of freeways, streets, bridges, and tunnels. Very quickly you're completely disoriented, confused, and lost. You're not quite sure what's happening. You thought you were good with directions, but nothing is making sense. What the map says isn't reflecting what you're seeing in front of you. You finally realize you have the wrong map; you had pulled out the map of Chicago. Once you get the correct map of NYC out, everything makes sense, and you're able to navigate to your final destination.

Most people are confused and disoriented because they don't have the right life map, a model and associated process, to get from where they are to their desired destination, their Greatest Life. They keep trying with their old model but, as hard as they try each time, it doesn't work. As the saying goes, "The definition of insanity is doing the same thing over and over and expecting different results."

This was my dilemma for many years . . . until I discovered a new life model. With this major shift to a "true" perspective, life finally made sense. Real transformation was possible using this model to guide the way!

I-MODEL . . . A NEW FRAMEWORK FOR YOUR JOURNEY

In I-Lignment, the conceptual framework is the I-Model. It gives I-Lignment structure. The I-Lignment process is the actual transformational journey, with the I-Model putting into context your current life as well as how to navigate from where you are to your Greatest Life.

I've realized through my life experience that the most powerful ideas are based on the simplest models. The purpose of the I-Model is to bring simplicity and clarity to the complex and confusing world of personal transformation.

The I-Model has seven components:

- The Shell
- The Impact of Time
- The Now
- The "I"ntersection
- The Void
- The Journey Inward to "I"
- The Shift of Source

In the remainder of this chapter, I'll discuss each component of the I-Model. In the following two chapters, the I-Model will be used to put in context each step of the I-Lignment process. This will provide a significant Shift of Perspective critical for your transformational journey.

THE SHELL

THE CURRENT "YOU" CREATED OUTSIDE-IN

Who you are today is your "shell." The chapter "Why? Why Is My Life Like This?" explained in detail the development of this shell and how it impacts your life experience when living in and from the shell.

> NOTE: If you haven't already, please read "Why? Why Is My Life Like This?" It's important for understanding this concept.

Your shell is a combination of your body that encapsulates your emotions, thoughts, beliefs, and stories that have accumulated over time . . . mostly coming from the outside-in. When an event happens in your life, thoughts are formed, followed by an emotional reaction or the reverse, an emotion occurs followed by thoughts. If the emotions or thoughts are strong enough, a belief (a mental-emotional construct) is formed about what happened, and you form a conscious or unconscious attachment to it. Over time, the combination of beliefs, thoughts, and strong emotions form stories about your life in an effort to explain your life circumstances as well as your behavior and appearance. You use all things and people outside of you to do this. Once we accept the external interpretation of things, most of the time they become permanent . . . even if the meaning may be distorted or untrue. All of this combines to influence how you show up in the world today and shapes your future.

As your shell continues to develop, it pulls you further

and further away from the core of your authentic self and into the world of the past and future . . . into a world of inauthenticity manufactured by others. It gets thicker and denser until it's all you can see; you become trapped in the shell. Even though it feels very solid and real, it's really a thin veneer covering who you really are.

You're also separated from true relationships with others and the world around you. As you interact with others, your inauthentic shell is bumping up against their inauthentic shell. Neither person can see beyond the shell inward to their own authentic self, let alone see through to the authentic self of the other person. The shells block any type of true, authentic relationship.

A simple metaphor is an eagle egg. It's hard and brittle and it's all you can see. You think the eagle, at that point in its life, is the outer shell of the egg. The eagle's only experience is inside the shell. In reality, the shell is but a thin veneer hiding the majesty of the actual eagle.

Your shell is your "i" (small "i") . . . the inauthentic, small, and weak illusion separate from who you really are buried deep inside you. Everything you see in the outer world and everything you perceive about yourself is seen through and distorted by the contents of the shell.

YOUR CURRENT SOURCE

Your shell is your current source of your life. Since the quality of your life experience depends on the source of life you choose, you can now see why your life is the way it is. It reflects the contents of your shell, the input of which was derived from many convoluted, conflicted, and dysfunctional external sources over time. If all this is the case, would it be any surprise that the output of such a source—our emotions, thinking, words, and actions—be equally convoluted, conflicted, and dysfunctional? And that the quality of our life would be significantly impacted?

You'll never discover your Greatest Life living in and from the shell.

NOTE: Earlier in the book, I referred to the shell as the "fog." Throughout the rest of the book, I will call this inauthentic identity your "shell." I'll also interchangeably refer to it as the "i" . . . using lower case to denote it's the inauthentic self as opposed to the capitalized "I," which is the authentic self. You'll understand the importance of making this distinction as you proceed through the book.

THE IMPACT OF TIME

TIME DOESN'T EXIST . . . THE PAST AND FUTURE DON'T EXIST . . . THE ONLY REALITY IS NOW . . . THIS PRESENT MOMENT

This is an incredibly important concept to understand. It's fundamental to your ability to transform your life. The past is gone . . . it doesn't exist! The future isn't here yet . . . it doesn't exist! The only thing that is real is now . . . each present moment! And it's where all your power lies.

This is a foreign concept for most people, because we're raised to live in a world of time where the past is perceived to be so important and real. Our remembered past is used, with or without awareness, as the foundation to shape our imagined future.

All of this remembered past and imagined future are stored in your mind. As explained in the last section, "The Shell," as well as in the chapter "Why? Why Is My Life Like This?," this mind becomes part of your inauthentic shell. It's composed almost entirely of your remembered past and imagined future created from the outside-in. This is how we get trapped in a linear, time-based progression of life, stuck between the high walls of our own Grand Canyon of life. We're living the past forever . . . on autopilot.

Your mind is constantly pulling you into this past or future and taking you away from the reality of the present moment . . . the only place a real life can be lived and where your Greatest Life can be discovered.

Crazy thing is . . . the past and future don't even exist. It's only you that give them any power by carrying them forward in your mind. If this is true, then much of your shell doesn't exist either. It's based on things that don't exist right now . . . in the reality of this present moment.

When people say, "living the dream," it takes on a whole new meaning. They're speaking truth. They really are living in a dream, living an illusion of a past that is gone and a future that isn't here yet.

You'll never discover your Greatest Life living in time.

THE NOW . . . WHERE ALL POWER LIES

THE PRESENT MOMENT IS THE ONLY "TIME" THAT'S REAL!
Understanding, fully accepting, and living the truth that the only thing that exists is the now, this present moment, are critical. The past doesn't exist. How can it when it happened already and, right after it happened, it was gone, leaving you in the next present moment? Anything that resembles the past is something that you have chosen to carry into your new present moment as an emotion, belief, or story. It isn't real; it's just a memory in your mind. The future isn't here yet; it's just a story of what might happen. It isn't real; it's just a thought in your mind. Once the future finally gets here and becomes reality, it is the present.

It's always the present moment . . . the now! Time means nothing; living life in the present moment means everything! It allows you to have a fresh start in each moment . . . with a beginner's mind.

This concept took me a while to get my arms around. Besides being a "transforming lives" coach, I'm an entrepreneur, developing businesses that transform lives. In developing businesses, I do business plan development and strategic planning. I've been doing both all my life in various careers. When I first heard the concept that the past and future didn't exist and only the present moment was real, it didn't seem possible. But after I really understood and accepted it, I realized how often I was living in the remembered "past" or envisioned "future" . . . and completely missing the incredible life happening all around me in that moment!

When you experience living now, your world around you comes fully alive. As I've been writing this book on the Oregon Coast, mostly overlooking the Pacific Ocean, I've been acutely attuned to staying present. The magnificent beauty of each present moment all around me is amazing . . . the roar of the waves as they crest and tumble toward shore, then crash against the rocky cliffs, sending spray high toward the sky . . . seagulls soaring gracefully in the currents of the wind . . . the feel of the strong onshore breeze on my face as it rocks my car . . . blue sky transitioning to gray clouds and then rain . . . early-morning fog dissipating off the ocean cliffs . . . birds pulling mussels from the rocks and then dropping them on the same rocks to break them open for a feast . . . seafoam on the shoreline, breaking off and being carried off in the wind . . . the rise of the high tide as it floods the small bay and then retreats into the ocean at low tide . . . the back spray off the tops of large waves artistically curling back into the next wave. I'm able to fully experience all of this and much more by being fully present and not being absorbed in a mind of the past and future that would not allow the reality of my amazing experience right now.

You're so consumed trying to escape from the past and chase the promise of a better future, you don't see the vibrant life right in front of you. You feel something is missing in your life . . . so you continue to search for answers in time. As you do, life becomes *less* . . . less alive, less empowered, less connected, less loving, less free, less joyful, less passionate, less abundant. You'll never find what you're looking for by dwelling on the past or dreaming about the future. What you've always been looking for can be found by being in presence, internally and externally, in each new present moment.

You have a choice. You can be pulled out of reality by a focus on time or you can BE present where it's possible to live a real life. Always make the decision for living a life now! Be real!

THE PRESENT MOMENT IS WHERE ALL YOUR TRUE POWER LIES!

The past and future don't exist; therefore, they have no real power. How can they? It's only in your mind that you give them the illusion of power to influence your life. Anytime you get pulled out of the present moment by a focus on the past or future, it weakens you.

In addition, as explained in the chapter "Why? Why Is My Life Like This?," you gave away your power to others as your current life, your shell, was created from the outside-in. As you continue to live from your shell, you continue to give away your power, rendering yourself weak and controlled.

The only place you'll reclaim your inherent power is right now . . . in this present moment. It's the only place you can live a real life and take action. It's also the only time where you can journey inward to tap into your inner source of power and start creating and living a powerful life from the inside-out. It's the key that unlocks the door to your Greatest Life!

The time for beginning your transformation is now! It is always only now!

You'll find your Greatest Life only by being present.

THE "I"NTERSECTION

"Who am I?" is answered at the "I"ntersection of your life . . . at your authentic "I."

It's at the core of your life, at your very center. It's where time shrinks to only the present moment. It's where you move inward past your shell to a point in space that is no longer impacted by the accumulation of all your dysfunctional past and restricted, fearful future. It's tapped into your Inner Source of Life with unlimited power and creativity. It's where you discover your True Purpose. It's the launching pad for designing a whole new way of life . . . your Greatest Life!

Right now, your authentic "I" is hidden deep inside you . . . covered up by your shell. The great news is, even though you can't see or experience it yet, your "I" already exists . . . and is waiting for you to uncover it. It's like the sun hidden by clouds; you can't see it, but you know it's there and will burn through the clouds eventually, allowing its brilliance to shine on the world.

The "I"ntersection is at the center of the I-Model and is the first destination of the I-Lignment journey. Before you can discover your Greatest Life, you must first uncover your authentic self, your "I."

EVERYTHING YOU'VE BEEN LOOKING FOR OUT THERE . . . IS AT YOUR "I"NTERSECTION

Once there, the inherent core attributes of the "I"ntersection are yours—true freedom, a deep peace, unconditional love, contentment, an ongoing sense of joy, and an Inner Power. You don't just have these attributes; you become them. You are freedom. You are deep peace. You are unconditional love. You are contentment. You are radiant joy. You are power from within. Since you ARE these attributes, you don't have to give them away to specific people; rather, you radiate them indiscriminately to the world around you.

Think about all the effort you've made over many years pursuing freedom, peace, love, contentment, joy, and a sense of personal power out there in the world. Think about the degree of success you've had making any of them a reality in your life. You'll never find them, at least consistently, while living in and from your shell. Isn't it amazing, all the while, they've been inside you already, waiting patiently for you?

These core attributes form a solid foundation for creating your new life. Because you're tapped into your inner creative source at the "I," true creativity will flow out from deep within you through these attributes to form the new, powerful you.

INFINITE DEGREES OF FREEDOM ... UNLIMITED POSSIBILITIES!

As you create your new life from "I," you have a newfound freedom you've never had before when trying to create from a life dictated by your past and future—a past and future that limited your options within the walls of a time-based linear path. Much of what you were creating for the future was an extension or "improvement" of what you had done before.

When you create from your "I"ntersection, after having freed yourself from the binds of time and escaped the prison of your shell, you have infinite degrees of freedom from that point in space. You have the flexibility to go in any direction and have access to unlimited possibilities. From here, you can create whatever life you want authentically ... from the inside-out!

You'll discover your Greatest Life living in and from the "I"ntersection.

THE VOID

The void is the gap between your inauthentic shell "i" and your authentic "I," which is at the center of your life. It was formed as your life was created outside-in, pulling you away from your true self. When this happened, this gap started to be a source of dysfunction in your life.

LIFE OF DUALITY AND SEPARATION

The existence of both your authentic "I" and inauthentic "i" creates duality; there are two of you competing for attention. Duality comes into existence with the formation of the gap between "I" and "i" (or as you get separated from your authentic self). The more you live in time and make that the focus in your life, the bigger the gap becomes and the further you pull yourself away from who you are in truth. Right now, your inauthentic "i" is most likely winning the battle.

I'm sure you've heard people say, "I just don't feel whole." This duality and the gap created between authenticity and inauthenticity are the reason why. These people aren't whole . . . they're split. As long as you live in and from your separate shell, you'll never feel whole and will have a general sense of separation and emptiness.

Duality goes away and wholeness for yourself and oneness with others are discovered . . . when only "I," your authentic self, remains. Oneness with others, and how it comes about, will be explained later in the book.

ABANDONMENT

The void also causes feelings of abandonment. This is a big issue for many people. These feelings are caused, at the root, by your separation from your authentic self . . . from "I." You have abandoned the real you for an inauthentic persona.

You also feel abandoned in relationship with others because both of you are separated by each of your respective voids; you are only interacting with each other at the surface of life. You've abandoned other people while living in your shell, and other people have abandoned you while living in their shell. You've been separated from each other, lost in your respective fogs, especially at any level of authenticity.

You then create a strong belief: "I've been abandoned." In truth, everyone abandoned themselves as they entered the world of inauthenticity. This abandonment is only reflected and emphasized when interacting with others.

The feelings of abandonment go away when only "I," your authentic self, remains.

FEELINGS OF LACK AND EMPTINESS . . . SOMETHING'S MISSING

When you get separated from your authentic "I" as the void expands, you also get separated from what exists there as well: Unconditional love, peace, contentment, freedom, joy, and Inner Power. These powerful ways of being are replaced by the effects caused by dysfunctional contents of your shell as well as the emptiness of the void.

Out of this arise many of your insatiable wants and your pursuits to fulfill them. You're looking for something, any-thing, to fill the void, fix what appears to be broken in your shell, and make the pain go away. As you endlessly search out there to satisfy your wantings and have trouble fulfilling them, you create strong beliefs: I'm not lovable . . . I'll never find happiness . . . I've been abandoned . . . I'm powerless . . . I'll never find peace in my life . . . I'm not good enough . . . unconditional love doesn't exist . . . I need to find the right person to complete me . . . my life is empty. The list of wants, pursuits, and resulting beliefs is endless.

Most of the wants in your life will finally go away when only "I," your authentic self, remains.

You'll always be separated from your Greatest Life as long as the void exists.

THE JOURNEY INWARD TO "I"

If everything you're looking for in life is at, or can be created from, your "I"ntersection, then obviously the journey you need to take is inward. This journey takes you beyond your shell, collapsing the void, and immersing yourself at the center of your authentic life . . . at "I."

Starting Point	Ending Point
Your shell	Your "I"ntersection . . . "I"
Inauthenticity	Authenticity
Weakness	Inner Power
Conditional or imitation love	Unconditional Love
Chaos	Peace
Unhappiness	Joy
Unease	Contentment
Source of Life outside-in	Source of Life inside-out
Aimless	Clear Purpose
Limited options	Endless Possibilities

You've spent your whole life searching for a better life in the opposite direction . . . out there somewhere getting guidance from many others. Right now, if you're like so many people, you're disillusioned . . . dis-"i"-llusioned. Illusion means "a thing that is or is likely to be wrongly perceived or interpreted by the senses." Your disillusionment is because you are living in and from your shell "i"; you're living a life composed mostly of stuff that doesn't exist anymore (the past) and stuff that hasn't arrived yet (the future). It doesn't represent what's happening here . . . right now. This approach to life obviously hasn't worked all that well.

THE ONLY WAY IS THROUGH

The reverse direction is the answer and will dissolve your issues. The answer is not to add more illusion from the outside to the shell. Rather, it's an inner process of undoing what already exists that is blocking you from living an authentic life at your core. The only way to do this is to go through it, and the only direction you can take to go through it is within. It's the only direction you can take to transform your life . . . and life circumstances.

This is the first of two parts of the I-Lignment process. I'll take you through a description of this inward journey in the next chapter, "Journey to the 'I'ntersection."

THE TARGET IS A POINT IN SPACE THAT IS INFINITELY UNBOUNDED . . . "I"

Going within to your "I" . . . at the Intersection . . . is a dichotomy. It seems like you're shrinking to a small point, much smaller than who you are now. But when you move beyond your current shell inward to the "I"ntersection, you expand into something much greater and more powerful that you ever imagined possible, with infinite possibilities and with all the things you've been looking for . . . unlimited, unconditional love . . . peace . . . joy . . . freedom . . . purpose . . . and a passion for life.

You'll find your Greatest Life only through your inward journey to "I."

THE SHIFT OF SOURCE

YOU ARE ALWAYS CREATING . . . THE QUALITY OF YOUR LIFE DEPENDS ON YOUR CREATIVE SOURCE!

Up to this point, you've been "creating" your life using your shell and the world around you as your creative source. Think about what that means, especially now that you better understand how your current life was haphazardly thrown together by others. It can't be a surprise to you that the quality of your life, both internal and external, isn't quite where you want it.

The emotions, thoughts, beliefs, and stories in your shell generate thousands of thoughts, words, and actions. Most of them are automatic reactions, learned in the past, that get triggered by people and events in your external world. If the contents of your shell are dysfunctional, convoluted, and conflicted, then the thoughts, words, and actions will reflect this. None are neutral; they all create! They create your life . . . and create the world around you! Dysfunctional source . . . dysfunctional life . . . dysfunctional world.

You need to change your Source of Life if you want to transform your life. You need to shift to a Source of Life that empowers you to live inside-out. That source lies at the "I"ntersection of your life. Once you're living in and from your authentic "I," you're able to tap into this Inner Source.

Your Inner Source is like the depths of the Pacific Ocean. Right now, you're skimming the surface of the ocean in your pleasure craft, not realizing the riches that lie just below the surface. You may sense there's so much more to the body of water but, right now, you can't see or experience it. The ocean surface doesn't even begin to describe the vastness and life-empowering abundance of the ocean depths.

The shift to your new source occurs organically during the inward journey to "I" described briefly in the last section; how it happens will be described in more detail in the next chapter. This is the second of the Four Shifts of Personal Transformation: Shift of Source.

Your Greatest Life is possible only by shifting to your Inner Source of Life.

CREATING YOUR LIFE . . .
FROM YOUR TRUE "I"

Once you have uncovered and are living from your "I"ntersection, you've successfully escaped the Winchester Mystery House maze of your life, mentioned earlier in the book . . . a house constructed with no master plan.

You've uncovered a piece of fertile ground that will allow you to develop a new life. Instead of taking a bulldozer to the property to begin building yet another house with no plan, you now sit in the middle of the property in silence and listen for what the land is asking you to create. You open yourself up to any possibility and are guided by what you hear.

This is the fertile ground you want to get to for the second part of the I-Lignment journey, "Living Your Greatest Life . . . from 'I.'" From this point in space "I," and through your connection with your Inner Source of Life, anything is possible. If done right, it will guide you to the creation of your Greatest Life.

Let's see how you get to this fertile ground . . .

CHAPTER EIGHT:
JOURNEY TO THE "I"NTERSECTION

As I mentioned at the beginning of the book, I love nature . . . absolutely love nature! It's such a great teacher of life. I like to spend as much time out in it as possible, especially in wilderness areas. It was on one of my hikes in Yosemite National Park, burdened with a heavy backpack, that I conceived of this metaphor depicting this part of the I-Lignment journey:

Jeff had moved to Silicon Valley five years before to take on a software-development role in a high-tech start-up. Even though it was exciting at the beginning, the stress and loneliness of long work hours and high-pressure development schedules, as well as the chaotic feel of the fast-moving city around him, was taking its toll. He was close to a breaking point.

He decided to leave the city for a week and get out into nature to unwind and reflect on his life, something he used to do often but had neglected for many years. He went into his garage and dug out his wilderness backpack, which he always kept prepared for the next hike. It seemed much heavier than he remembered, but he figured it had everything he needed for this trip and threw it into the back of his car.

He drove 350 miles to the trailhead in the Klamath National Forest in Northern California and started descending through the forest into a very deep valley. As he tackled switchback after switchback, his journey seemed to get more difficult and overwhelming. He struggled with the weight of his backpack as he went through the forest that was getting darker and denser. His focus was on putting one foot in front of the other, just trying to make it down the trail without collapsing. His attitude wasn't improving but was getting much worse. This wasn't the relaxing adventure he had expected, nor the one he wanted.

As the trail began to parallel a beautiful, clear whitewater river, Jeff decided to take a break to sit on the bank of the river and rest. He opened his backpack, expecting to get out some snacks, but he found his backpack was actually full of rocks of all sizes. He then remembered he had been throwing all the unusual rocks he had been attracted to on other hikes over the years into the backpack. Unawares, he had been carrying them on this hike as a useless, heavy burden for the past fifteen miles.

With frustration, he took one of the rocks out and threw it into the river. He watched it tumble into the river and disappear in the fast current. He spent the next thirty minutes taking out more rocks and throwing them into the river.

When he picked up the backpack to continue down the trail, he noticed how much lighter the backpack was and how much more he was enjoying the hike and everything around him. Each day for the remainder of his trip, he would take breaks on the edge of the river and throw more of the rocks into the current. Each day his journey became lighter and more enjoyable. His awareness grew of the beauty and amazing life that was teeming all around him. He felt an increasingly deep sense of peace, love, and contentment for the nature he was immersed in. On the last day, he came across a section of the river where it flattened, became wider, and slowed. The surface was serene, peaceful, and smooth. He felt content just stopping and being still in this calm beauty.

Jeff had gotten rid of every rock except a small one. He took it out and threw it in. As it hit the water, he saw how greatly it disturbed the calm surface and disrupted the natural tranquility of that moment. He realized, as a powerful revelation, how much all the "rocks" in his life, which he had been inadvertently collecting and carrying around for years, had been negatively impacting him and dragging him down. In that moment, he made the commitment to get rid of all the rocks in his life and to live a life that would allow the beauty of each moment to shine through.

Your journey to the "I"ntersection is one of throwing the rocks of your life, of your shell, into the river in each present moment, allowing them to flow out of you and disappear. As you do consistently and with commitment, the real you, your authentic "I," begins to shine through.

As you go through this part of the I-Lignment process, you'll be doing something that is just the opposite of how you normally react. Up to this point, when you felt discomfort or that something was missing in your life, your immediate reaction was, most likely, to find something to fill the void, fix the issue by getting help out there in the world somewhere, or cover it up.

I-Lignment is different. It recognizes the path to your Greatest Life can't be started with a focus on anything outside of you and won't be fixed with yet another externally supplied "life patch." It's initially an inward journey through and beyond the shell by becoming aware of, and then letting go of, stuff that has built up over a lifetime, stuff that is keeping you stuck in your current inauthentic life. This dissipates the thickness and density of the shell, reduces its magnetic power over you, shrinks the void described earlier, and allows you to BE at the "I"ntersection of your life . . . "I." At the end of your inward journey, you have created a clearing for your new life possibility to germinate within, and an authentic life to emerge. You've escaped a life lived outside-in to a life that is emerging from the inside-out.

TARGETING REAL TRANSFORMATION . . . CAUSE NOT EFFECT

Imagine your life is a movie. The current script of your movie is the contents of your shell being projected out onto the screen of the world. If you don't like the movie you're seeing and try to change the images on the world screen, nothing really happens. To make any real changes, you need to go back to the creator of the movie, the scriptwriter, and make the changes to the script with them. If the script writer is egotistical and is unwilling to change the script, then it's imperative you choose another writer.

There's a concept captured in the above metaphor that

you need to be fully conscious of and embrace. It's a critical part of your transformation and will help you assume total responsibility for your journey. It's the concept of "cause and effect." Whenever we have any life experience, there is always a cause and an effect associated with it.

As you grew up, you were taught, by mostly unconscious people lost in their own shell, that your experience in life is the result of something outside of yourself. You may have been taught to expect negative experiences and to be prepared to react appropriately. This is especially true if you are raised in a victim-mentality environment or with many negative things happening to you throughout your life. You, therefore, believe the cause of all the negative in your life is something outside of you in the world . . . a person, a group of people, a current or historical event, or a specific situation. For that matter, you're also taught that all your positive experiences are because of something outside of yourself as well.

What you aren't taught is the truth. That you're 100 percent responsible for your overall life experience. It's a reflection of what's going on inside of your shell . . . your current source of life. This is a hard concept to swallow because you've been taught to blame someone or something out there for how you experience life. You're taught the cause is out there and the effect is what's happening to you; the reality is that the cause is the content of your shell, and the effect is what you see in the world around you. Another way of saying it is, the cause of your overall life circumstances is your inner emotional and mental makeup.

This is important for one big reason. If the cause is out there by another person, persons, or event, there's nothing you can do about it, and, therefore, you're a disempowered victim. But if the cause is within you, you're fully capable of changing it and are empowered to do so. Feel how the first false perspective is weak and hopeless . . . while the second true perspective is powerful and hopeful. With the first perspective, you'll never be in position to transform your life; with the second perspective, you absolutely are.

I-Lignment embraces the true concept of cause and effect and uses it throughout the process. This is especially true as you start to look at your current life and journey inward through and beyond your shell. If you know the causes of your current life issues are within the shell, you'll be looking in the right place to resolve them as you journey inward to "I."

In addition, understanding the true concept of cause and effect will help you shift to a new Source of Life. If your current source, your shell, isn't causing the type of life you want, why would you continue to live from that same source. You need to get rid of it and choose a new Source of Life that will cause your Greatest Life to be lived from the inside-out.

EXPERIENTIAL JOURNEY INWARD

For this to happen, you need to be fully engaged physically, emotionally, and mentally. This isn't a journey you take with only your mind. In fact, you can't think your way out of your current life. Thinking only keeps you in your mind and is an inhibitor to your progress, since it's your current thoughts, beliefs, and stories, along with their associated emotions, you're releasing as they arise.

The inward journey is an experiential journey where you literally feel your way through and beyond the maze of your current life. You need to experience your way out.

During your inward journey, you'll allow the causes of your current life experience, within your shell, to be triggered naturally in your daily life, and then be in position to see them, hear them, and ultimately release them. When the negative internal cause is gone, the effects you see in your life will magically disappear and be transformed. This is a logical and simple process of releasing internal obstacles. With consistent focus on this process, your direct path to "I" will gradually, sometimes suddenly, be unblocked.

UNCOVER THE FOUNDATION FOR YOUR GREATEST LIFE ... "I"

Once you've reached the "I"ntersection at your very core, you've successfully created a new clearing for your new life, with an underlying foundation of bedrock. It's solid and real . . . yet unbounded with unlimited possibilities. You've shifted from your weak, inauthentic shell as your source of life to your new Inner Source of Life. You will have completed the second Shift of Personal Transformation . . . the Shift of Source.

When you reach this point, you're truly free to create . . . whatever life you want!

This journey inward has five steps that are essential for getting to your final destination "I."

- Be Present . . . Now
- Body/Emotions/Mind Awareness
- Creating Separation
- Dissolving the Shell
- Shift of Source

Now let's go through each step of your journey to "I" . . .

BE PRESENT . . . NOW

The only place you can start your I-Lignment journey is right now . . . in the present moment. There is no other time where it's possible. The reason most people are not successful in transforming their lives is they remain stuck in time . . . embroiled in the past and future of their shell. They never find the "now" entry point for their inward journey.

When you bring all your attention solely on the present, you can literally have a momentary experience of your authentic "I" . . . the goal of "Journey to the 'I'ntersection." As you quiet your mind and its focus on the past and future, you drop below your shell to the "I"ntersection of your life and have an experience involving the attributes of "I" . . . unconditional love, a deep peace, true freedom, contentment, joy, and timelessness. You may already have had glimpses of this during inspirational moments in your life.

A common experience is when you first truly fall in love with another person. Your world revolves around that person. Nothing else matters. When you're with the person, time seems to stand still. The past and future don't matter; what matters is each precious moment you're together. There's no judgment, only unconditional love. You are content just being with that person. Both of you have dropped below your shells, in each present moment you're together, and have connected at the level of your authentic "I"s.

Even though developing the ability to "be present" is a critical part of your transformational journey, it's important to not overcomplicate it. Being present can be accomplished by simply being present with something with you in that moment. It could be a flower, a tree, or a fire hydrant that you focus on to bring yourself to be present. In the case of a more formal approach, described later in "Your Transformation Journey," its focus is often on your breath, which is always present with you no matter where you go.

No matter the technique you choose, the purpose is to aid you to stay in the present and out of your time-based mind to facilitate an increased awareness of what is truly going on inside you, as well as around you. Once you're present with an inward focus, you can more clearly see the internal causes of your external life experience (cause and effect) as they get triggered. This is the beginning of transforming your life.

PULLED OUT OF "NOW"

Being present ever so briefly is easy. Again, it can be as simple as focusing on something present with you in that moment and quieting the mind. What's more difficult is staying present as a fundamental way of life.

Your shell is like a powerful magnet. It yanks you right back out of being present into its world of your remembered past and projected future. If you're to remain present through the process of transformation and beyond, you need to have new transformation tools to help you both stay present and reduce the magnetic pull of the shell.

A STILL, QUIET SPACE . . . FOR TRANSFORMATION

Trying to transform while in the noisy, confusing, dysfunctional, time-based space of your shell without changing anything is like trying to lift yourself up by your bootstraps . . . impossible. Your mind's constant chatter gets in the way of seeing what's in your way. The transformation tools you choose to aid you in your journey need to give you the ability to get past your mind chatter and into a still, quiet place . . . whenever needed and wherever you are. From this quiet place, you can clearly see the parts of your shell that most affect you and that need attention in each present moment.

"MEDITATION" AND "RELEASE" ARE THE TWO POWERFUL TOOLS!

I'm sure you've had an experience like this at some point in your life: You're hiking in the woods on a beautiful, warm day, consumed in thought, and come across a small pond that is perfectly still and serene, with a surface like glass. You stop, get quiet, and let the experience soak into your senses. You feel a deep sense of peace and calm like you've never felt before. Time disappears, and what's happening right now is all that matters. You'd like this experience to go on forever. Then large gas bubbles rise to the water's surface from the bottom of the pond, shattering the surface with circular ripples extending in all directions. The peace and calm are gone for the moment. You clearly see the impact of this event on the pond and your own feeling of peace and well-being. Out of curiosity, you begin wondering what caused the bubbles.

This illustrates meditation's two primary roles in the I-Lignment process. First, meditation brings all your attention to the present moment, quiets the mind, and creates a calm space. As you now know, this is critical because the now is the only place you can start and continue your transformational journey inward. Second, meditation allows the "bubbles" in your life (body sensations, emotions, thoughts, beliefs, and stories) to rise into your awareness in this calm space to be clearly seen and heard . . . and then released. This releasing reduces the thickness and density of your shell and, over time, dissipates it, allowing you to go beyond it inward to be in and live from your "I"ntersection . . . "I."

NOTE: It's important right now to mention that meditation is a tool. Some people get hung up on the concept of "meditation." Please don't! Treat it as a tool—no more, no less—when used during the process of I-Lignment.

Being present is experienced in Part Five: "Your Transformation Journey," in the section "Be Present . . . Now!"

Once perfected, being present becomes a powerful ally in your transformation throughout the I-Lignment process . . . and then evolves into a powerful way of life.

"BODY/EMOTIONS/MIND" AWARENESS

As mentioned in the chapter "Why? Why Is My Life Like This?," your shell is the sum total of all your thoughts, beliefs, stories, and emotions collected over your lifetime, mostly sourced from the outside-in, and then stuffed into your body. Because you have, for most of your life, looked outside yourselves for input, you increasingly lose touch with what is going on inside of you within your shell. It's quite crazy you do this, because your shell is and continues to be the current source of your life.

HIDDEN YET STILL IMPACTING YOU

You especially have lost touch with your innermost emotions. If you recall, during the end of the second phase of the development of your life—around the age of seven, when you entered school—there was a shift from emotional-mental development to mental-physical development. You may have been encouraged to stop being so emotional and to use your mind to think your way through life. Your emotional development slowed considerably and perhaps even stopped. You may have been emotionally stunted, with most of your emotions hidden beneath the surface of your everyday awareness. The same is true for many of your beliefs and stories . . . especially those that were painful and were, therefore, suppressed into your subconscious.

To this day, all your emotions, beliefs, and stories are still being triggered and impacting your life experience, yet many of them remain hidden from your awareness.

I'll never forget the experience I had in my midthirties at a personal development workshop in San Diego. We were learning an emotion-release technique and, therefore, needed to get in touch with our emotions during the first half day. People had varying degrees of success. Some were totally in touch with their emotions out of the gate; others gained greater awareness through the exercise; some struggled and made some progress. But the ones who amazed me were four men, about the age of my dad, who could not even feel one emotion. They finally got frustrated and left the workshop. It was wise they did because, without awareness of their emotions, they wouldn't have been successful in making any real changes that weekend.

Being aware of your emotions is critical! Strong emotions can create thousands, perhaps millions, of thoughts and stories that impact your life. Trying to change your life by focusing on your thoughts is tough, because the moment you change one thought, the underlying emotional cause creates more. Transformation requires getting to the original cause . . . your underlying emotions and beliefs.

REJUVENATE YOUR AWARENESS . . . BODY, MIND, EMOTIONS

To rapidly progress in your transformational journey, you must enhance your awareness of the content and activity within your shell. After all, how can you transform what you don't even know exists and is hidden from your view. You need to create the ability to be aware of your emotions and the associated thoughts/beliefs/stories so you can, when they arise in your life, experience them, hear their message, and then release them.

To develop this awareness in I-Lignment, you'll do a meditation that starts with physical awareness followed by mental and emotional awareness. The physical awareness part of the meditation brings you to the present and gets you in touch with your body so you can feel its sensations. The emotional and mental awareness part of the meditation allows you to feel your emotions, within your body, as well as connect with the related beliefs.

Body/Emotions/Mind Awareness is experienced in Part Five: "Your Transformation Journey," in the section "Increase Body/Emotions/Mind Awareness."

Awareness of arising emotions and beliefs gives you the fuel for transformation.

CREATING SEPARATION

When I first started going down the path of my own transformation, I had the fortune of meeting a spiritual coach in a coffee shop. I asked her, "If you had one piece of advice to give me, what would that be?" She said, "Get out of yourself." That was all she said. I was perplexed. It wasn't until much later that the power of that one sentence made sense. She was, in essence, telling me to get out of my shell . . . my small "i."

Your true transformation is a process of "undoing," "releasing," and "letting go of" the inauthentic person you have become to create a clearing for the emergence of your greatest self from your authentic "I."

If you react like I did, this all sounds great until you begin to feel huge inner resistance because it appears you're starting down a path that has a goal of eliminating *you*. How can you possibly eliminate the very thing you think you are? It feels like a death sentence. This resistance is exacerbated if you read Eastern spiritual philosophy and other books that say you end up in a place of emptiness or nothingness. Who wants to go through all that inner personal work, letting go of the certainty of who you are right now, to end up in a big, empty void of nothingness? A natural human reaction is to hang on to what you know is certain or familiar in your life and shy away from uncertainty. The unknown is scary and creates feelings of fear.

You won't "get out of yourself" if it's all you think you are.

EXPERIENCING SEPARATION

It's critical you get to the point where you know you are much greater than just your limited shell. That, in fact, the shell is blocking you from realizing your greatest self.

There are three ways used during I-Lignment to successfully create separation from your current identification with your shell and experience a sense of your true self. The first two ways are intellectually, and the third is a felt experience.

Intellectually

First, it's important to realize what you're not. You are not your inauthentic shell. This is a big reason I wrote the chapter "Why? Why Is My Life Like This?" It helps you understand your current life, how it all came about, and that its source of development was mostly from others . . . a life created from the outside-in. It's what others wanted you to become. In essence, it's not your creation; it's their creation.

Second, it's equally important to envision what's waiting for you out of and beyond your shell—a life lived in and from your authentic "I." This is the reason I wrote Chapter Five, "Living Life Powerfully . . . from the Inside-Out," and Chapter Ten, "The Transformed You." Both paint the picture of how life is when living an authentic life inside-out.

The first intellectual insight gives you incentive and reasons to move away from a life lived in and from the shell. The second pulls you toward a life that is infinitely better.

Felt Experience

The third way to create separation from your shell is to literally feel yourself expand beyond your shell through a powerful I-Lignment meditation. The meditation will allow you to break free from the prison of your shell and feel yourself energetically extending way beyond your body into a much more expansive and spacious state. From this point, you can look back at your inauthentic self (your shell) as an observer. You'll realize the expanded state you've experienced during the meditation is who you are, in reality, and that your limited, dysfunctional, and inauthentic shell is not.

As you increasingly experience the real you and its inherent attributes of deep peace, unconditional love, true freedom, and joy, you'll be more willing to let go of the shell bit by bit as the emotions and beliefs come up to be heard and then released.

You can experience this separation from your inauthentic

self in Part Five: "Your Transformation Journey," in the section "Create Separation . . . Going Beyond Your Shell.

Now you can release and transform from a powerful point of view . . .

DISSOLVING THE SHELL

A hoarder's house is an accumulation of stuff collected over the years. There's no rhyme or reason for how it was collected; it just happened. They got stuff handed down from family members; they bought cheap stuff at the local thrift store; they found stuff abandoned along the road; they got many presents over the years; they kept all the old books and magazines because they thought they might need to refer to them someday. As a result, their house is unlivable, with narrow pathways that constrict movement. It smells moldy and the tall stacks of junk threaten to topple at any time and crush them. It makes it hard for them to organize and live an effective life. Hopefully, they wake up one day and realize how difficult and unmanageable their life has become and are more than ready to change; they commit to clean house and use their reclaimed home as a launching pad into a new life.

You're the hoarder of your life, and this is the pivotal moment to start cleaning your internal house.

Everything so far in this "Journey to the 'I'ntersection" is designed to prepare you for this moment. You develop the ability to bring yourself present, out of your time-based mind, and into a quiet, calm space; you develop the ability to be keenly aware of what is happening within you physically, mentally, and emotionally; and you develop the ability to separate yourself from your shell so you can look back at it objectively, as an observer, realizing it isn't really you, but rather a manufactured person created by others.

You're now ready to begin the process of releasing the parts of your shell that come up as you go about your daily life. With consistent and committed focus, you'll begin to dismantle the shell. It will get less dense, more transparent, and have less controlling power over you. I like to call this process "uncovery" (versus *recovery*) because it's descriptive of what's happening. You're going through a process of uncovering what's been hidden inside you all along . . . the real you.

UNCOVERY . . . DISCOVERING AND RELEASING THE "CAUSES"

If you think about your daily life, trillions of things are happening around you constantly. You're aware of a minute fraction of them. Of the things you're aware of, most are neutral; you sense them but have no vested interest in them. They're there but you don't really care. But then there are those people, events, or objects that really catch your attention, especially the ones that trigger you in a powerful, negative, emotional way. You need to begin to see these as opportunities for your personal transformation; the seed for transformation lies right in the middle of your reaction.

A typical way you have reacted to these life events has been to project blame outside of yourself for the negative feelings and thoughts you're having "as a result of" the experience.

Or, if you couldn't do that, you would resort to any number of the other coping mechanisms discussed in the chapter "Why? Why Is My Life Like This?" . . . accept, ignore, reject, escape, project, suppress, or cover up. But now you know these approaches don't help you but, instead, keep you stuck.

Rather than cope, you need to respond by metaphorically welcoming that triggered reaction into your house for a cup of tea and a chat so you can hear what it wants to tell you. Once you hear the message, you can open the door, say goodbye, and let it go on its way. The powerful transformation tool that allows you to welcome the reaction into your house for a cup of tea and a chat with you is "meditation." The powerful transformation tool that allows you to open the door, say goodbye, and let it go on its way is "release." Both tools are critical for "dissolving the shell."

As you put out the welcome mat during meditation, you'll find the reactions that come knocking at your door will fall into one of the four main categories of your shell's content: emotions, thoughts, beliefs, and stories.

Emotions: Emotions can exist by themselves. At some point in your life, you may have had an emotional experience that wasn't attached to anything else. This can happen early in your life before you start communicating with others and were just experiencing physical sensations and emotions. Emotions are energetically powerful by themselves, and they also put power behind and bring to life anything they are attached to, including thoughts, beliefs, and stories.

Thoughts: You have thousands of thoughts spinning around in your head every day. In fact, much of your constant mental chatter is composed of thoughts that mean something to you but for which you have little emotional attachment. However, the meaning you attached to the thought can still have an impact on your life . . . even without much emotion behind it.

Beliefs: Beliefs are what I call emotional-mental constructs. They can occur two ways. Either a thought about something comes first and then an emotion is attached to empower the thought, or the reverse: an emotion happens followed by attached thoughts to explain the emotion. In either case, strong emotions are the real power behind the belief.

Stories: Stories are combinations of emotions, thoughts, and beliefs that you put together to try to explain part of your life circumstances. Once again, the power behind the story are the emotions.

It's important you understand the above, because you need to know where to place your focus to be most effective in your personal transformation . . . especially during this phase of "Dissolving the Shell."

Trying to transform your life focused on releasing thoughts is like sticking your finger in one hole in a dam with a thousand leaks. One emotion or belief can generate thousands of thoughts. If you focus on releasing one thought, many more will be produced to replace it. Trying to change your thinking without first getting to the real cause is an exercise in futility.

The challenge of trying to release stories is similar. Since stories are composed of many emotions, thoughts, and beliefs, trying to release the story as the "cause," especially if it's complex and involved, is extremely difficult. The story isn't the root cause; in fact, it may contain many root causes.

The common element and power behind each are the emotions. This is important as you pursue identifying and releasing on the underlying cause of each reaction in your life. All of them (emotions, thoughts, beliefs, stories) impact your life, but the two that have the biggest impact are your inhibiting emotions and associated beliefs. When you focus on releasing them, you effectively release so much more, including thoughts and stories.

There are two important perspectives to shed light on at this point . . .

1. **Inhibiting Emotions and Inhibiting Beliefs:** I use the phrases "inhibiting emotions" and "inhibiting beliefs" rather than negative emotions and beliefs. It's obvious that "negative" emotions and beliefs can negatively impact you and keep you stuck, but so can "positive" emotions and beliefs. For example, if drinking alcohol makes you feel loving, then that positive emotion of love and the associated belief that alcohol makes you a loving person are coping mechanisms and will keep you stuck in your shell. It's a natural tendency to want to get rid of the negative in your life and keep the positive. But that perspective will not serve you well. When you look at the emotions and beliefs that come up in your life, you need to ask, not if they are positive or negative, but rather if they're inhibiting your journey to your Greatest Life. If so, then go through the process of releasing them.

2. **Being a Victim:** We live in a world where being a victim is in vogue; don't buy into it. This is one of the biggest inhibitors to transformation; you're defeated before you even begin.

Being victimized is a verb. It tragically happens to many people in many forms at some point in their life. It's real. It's tragic. It needs to be dealt with immediately and, if there's a perpetrator, they need to pay the consequences.

But being a victim is a noun. It's a choice of bringing "being victimized" into your life and making it part of who you are. You're adding to the thickness and density of your shell with strong emotions, one or more beliefs, and typically a powerful story. While you're doing this, you disempower yourself. For you to change at that point, something outside of you needs to change first . . . or so you and others believe. The stronger the emotions associated with it and the more it's supported by others, the harder it is to release . . . especially as the story becomes more and more of who you are. It becomes a major area of stuckness in your life, and you continue to be victimized over and over and over again . . . in your mind.

It's only when you let go of "being a victim" that you live from your power and escape the hold of the person who victimized you.

Discover and release your emotions and beliefs behind each of your reactions to dissolve the shell.

INTEGRATING TRANSFORMATION INTO YOUR DAILY LIFE

The I-Lignment process is designed to integrate into your daily life, allowing transformation to occur naturally, in a way that is sustainable. The process creates opportunities for life around you to mirror where you need to focus your attention internally. This is especially important during the process of dissolving the shell; it's most effective if you develop an innate ability to be open and aware so you allow emotions and beliefs to easily come into your awareness to be seen, heard, and then released as they happen.

There are three ways this is done throughout the I-Lignment process:

Meditation and Release ... During Self-Assessment

At the beginning of I-Lignment, you'll go through a quick self-assessment. The intent is to understand where you are and to explore what might be holding you back. I sometimes refer to this as an as-is assessment. This is to be done at least once at the beginning of the process, but it can be used as a tool at any time throughout your I-Lignment journey to determine your progress and identify any areas you need to focus on. Once you identify inhibiting emotions and beliefs during this assessment, you can begin practicing releasing them.

This self-assessment is experienced in Part Five: "Your Transformation Journey," in the section "I-Lignment Step Three—Ask Where am "i"?"

Meditation and Release ... During Dedicated Times Daily

When you start I-Lignment, it's important to have set times when you're committed to focus on transformation using the tools of meditation and release. Ideally this is done first thing in the morning and just before you go to bed.

These formal daily sessions are important for several reasons. First, they help you develop your ability to use the tools of meditation and release effectively. Second, they give you at least two concentrated times during the day to practice "being present," which is difficult at the beginning because you're so used to being lost in time. Third, they create dedicated periods every day to allow things to come up to be heard and then released. Fourth, they create a quiet time each day so you can hear your Inner Guidance, a critical part of living a life from the inside-out.

Meditation and Release ... During Everyday Life

Meditation and release at specific times daily is a great place to start, but the ultimate goal is to have them as tools you can use whenever and wherever needed.

Life doesn't wait until specific times on your schedule to trigger your conscious and unconscious emotions and beliefs.

As you well know, they happen randomly anytime. It's most effective if you take advantage of those triggering moments when they occur as a recognized opportunity to further your transformation.

In that exact moment, meditation can bring you present and into a place of centered, calm awareness. From this place, you can allow whatever is bothering you to come into clear focus, hear what it's trying to tell you, and then release it. This way, you deal with the emotion or belief before it starts spinning out of control with thousands of irrelevant thoughts and stories.

I-LIGNMENT RELEASE TOOLS

When the emotions and beliefs come to the surface to be seen and heard, you need the ability to effectively release them. This is where many people who have started down the path of personal development and transformation have failed. If you bring emotions or beliefs to the surface, especially if they're painful, and you have no way to release them, they'll eventually overwhelm you and you'll quit. The only thing you'll have accomplished is the awareness that they do exist, but they remain in the shell because they had no path of escape. The tools of transformation—meditation *and* release—must be used together to be successful at dissolving your shell.

There are four release techniques developed for use throughout I-Lignment. You'll be able to try all of them as you go through "Part Five: Your Transformation Journey." Eventually, you'll pick the ones that work best for you.

- I-Lignment Release Technique #1: i-Release
- I-Lignment Release Technique #2: The Why
- I-Lignment Release Technique #3: I-Flow
- I-Lignment Release Technique #4: I-Forgive

Each of these techniques is shown in Appendix C, "I-Lignment Meditation and Release Techniques," in written format. They're also available in coach-guided recorded audio format (see web link in Appendix C).

> NOTE: There are many other ways to "release" emotions and beliefs. The techniques presented above are ones I've found to be very effective, fit well into the I-Lignment process, and are easy to use in daily life.

THE VEIL OF FOG LIFTS

As you continue to release using these techniques, the fog of your inauthentic life will begin to dissipate. Where there was darkness, you begin to see light. Where you felt denseness, you begin to feel spaciousness. Where you were experiencing chaos, you begin to have clarity. Where you felt anxiousness, you begin to feel peace. Where you felt split, you begin to feel wholeness. Where you were aimless, you begin to sense purpose. Where you felt constrained, you begin to feel freedom. Where you felt hate, you begin to feel love.

The magnetic pull of your shell begins to weaken and has less influence over your life. Your ability to stay present, not being pulled into the past or future, strengthens. Your transformation increases its pace on your journey to "I."

INWARD TO HIGHER CONSCIOUSNESS AND INNER POWER

I'm sure you've heard the terms "consciousness" and "unconsciousness." Some people are referred to as unconscious or with low consciousness, while other people are seen as being conscious or having higher consciousness. We use these terms, but what do they really mean? Let me explain them right now in terms of I-Lignment, since they relate to your journey inward.

While you're living in and from your shell, you're mostly living in your past or future. Both are an illusion because they don't exist right here, right now. They pull you away from the only reality that is in each new present moment. Since you're pulled away from the present, you're not really aware of what's happening around you. You're unconscious, or, if you're somewhat aware of the present, which is seen through the lens of your past and future, you're of low consciousness.

In I-Lignment, because you bring yourself to the present and break free of your time-based bonds of the shell, your inward journey to "I" is one of ever-increasing levels of consciousness. In the shell, your conscious energy is relatively low, with inherent emotions such as fear, regret, hatred, and guilt to name just a few. But as you break out of the prison of your shell and get closer to your "I"ntersection, the conscious energy gets very high, with inherent emotions such as unconditional love, a deep peace, and joy.

This increase in your consciousness is a natural outcome of releasing your shell on your inward path to "I." You naturally move toward ever-higher levels of awareness, energy, and power.

At some point on your journey, you will experience a critical shift . . .

SHIFT OF SOURCE

A woman had lived all her life in a city on the banks of a large river at the mouth of the ocean. It was well known that the river was highly polluted and not healthy. Yet she and everyone else in the city lived off that marine ecosystem, drinking the water, eating the fish, digging up clams, catching crabs, and recreating in the river. She knew her life in this environment wasn't good for her because she was getting sick often, but she continued to live there because it was the only life she knew. However, she'd heard how beautiful the area was near the headwaters of the river's origin, a pure life-giving spring.

One day, after being sick for a week, she decided to pull up stakes and head upriver to create a new life just downstream from the spring. On the way, she began to see how the many tributaries feeding into the river from agricultural lands, industrial areas, and cities had contributed to its polluted condition downstream. The more she traveled upstream, the clearer the water became. As soon as she climbed into the sparsely populated mountain wilderness area, she noticed that the polluted river made a dramatic shift to a beautiful, crystal-clear mountain stream. She realized she had made a wise choice to shift her life to this flow of water coming from a pure source.

As you continue on your journey to your "I"ntersection, to ever-higher levels of consciousness, you, too, will experience this shift. You will shift from your inauthentic "unhealthy" shell as your current source of life to a new "pure" Source of Life flowing from within. The shift may be gradual, or it may be sudden; it may be subtle, or it may be dramatic. In any case, it naturally happens, at some point, as you're going through the process of releasing your shell. While you're releasing your current source and decreasing its magnetic pull and impact on you, you're simultaneously uncovering your Inner Source and increasing its influence on your life.

You're probably asking yourself, "How do I know when I've made the shift and are starting to live from this new Source?" Here are some indicators:

- You start to feel an Inner Power you've never experienced before.
- Your guidance will reflect the attributes of the source. If it's influenced by your shell, it will reflect limitation, scarcity, conditional love, inauthenticity, fearfulness, uncertainty, guilt, neediness, revenge, attack, separation, and control. If it's influenced by your Inner Source, it will reflect unlimited possibility, unconditional love, peacefulness, authenticity, sense of freedom, abundance, certainty, calmness, and unity.
- The source will also be reflected in the type of phrases you use to describe your life. When you are living in and from your shell, your small "i," your language will reflect the contents of your shell: "i" am _____. You are thinking or saying phrases such as these: "i" am weak. "i" am not good enough. "i" am fearful. "i" am a victim. "i" hate you. "i" am abandoned. "i" am empty. "i" am hopeless. "i" am lost. "i" am controlled. "i" am limited in my options. When you're sourcing your life from deep

within, your language shifts to "I" AM _____. You are thinking or saying phrases such as these: "I" AM powerful. "I" AM sending love to all my friends. "I" AM loved. "I" AM very peaceful. "I" AM feeling in control. "I" AM free. "I" AM free to choose. "I" AM everything I need to be successful. "I" AM confident. "I" AM able to do anything I want in life.

- Another indicator is a decreased dependency on the outside world. When you go through the process of releasing on the things that cause you to seek validation from others, such as "wanting approval," your perceived reliance on them decreases. You seek the approval of others less and will spend less time looking to others to help you in making personal decisions. You'll increasingly look inward for guidance and answers.

- Most important, you start to experience internally what you have been seeking all your life from out there in the world somewhere: deep peace, unconditional love, and true freedom.

INNER SOURCE OF LIFE

The beautiful Heceta Head Lighthouse, on the Oregon Coast, is like the Inner Source on your journey inward. It's a beacon of light in the darkness and fog. When lost out in the ocean on a boat, you initially see only a faint light from the lighthouse in the distance, but as you follow the light, it gets stronger and stronger, ultimately leading you to its source. You'll have the same experience as you move closer to your

"I"ntersection; once you see a glimmer of light of your Inner Source, it will begin to guide your way to "I."

As you go through I-Lignment, this "Inner Source of Life" will be described in different ways: Inner Source, Inner Power, Higher Power, Universe, God. The names are different, but I personally think of them as different names for the same thing.

Use whatever name represents for you this same incredible infinite power that can be found at the core of who you are. Pick the name that resonates as truth to you as you go through I-Lignment.

The name may seem important to you, but the Inner Source becomes real only through uncovering it, experiencing it, and allowing it to start flowing through your life; it can't be experienced through thinking only.

FIND AND TRUST YOUR INNER VOICE

In the middle of your newfound inner peace and unconditional love, you'll start to hear Inner Guidance. It's an "Inner Voice" you need to cultivate and have grow in influence over your life. With it, you have a singular Inner Voice rather than the multitude of external "voices" (often conflicting and dysfunctional) coming from your shell and from the outside world. It's the one guide that will lead you in the creation of your Greatest Life.

It's important to understand that true integrity isn't about coming into alignment with a set of rules others have defined for you but, rather, it's about being in I-Lignment with the truth from within. If you're not trusting and following your Inner Guidance, then you're living out of integrity; you're living an inauthentic life.

As you cultivate this Inner Voice during the process of releasing your shell, you'll initially go from an uncertainty of whether to trust it, especially since you're still being greatly influenced by your shell and its multitude of external voices; to then trusting it with some reservations and wanting more proof it's true; and finally to a "knowing" that it's true and can be trusted implicitly, after you've been given enough proof that, if you had followed its guidance each time, it did or would have taken you down the right path. Getting to this point of trusting your Inner Voice is especially important for those times on your journey when you hear guidance that doesn't make sense to you in the moment, but you have a strong "knowing" that it's the right thing to do. With absolute trust, you can confidently follow the guidance anyway, "knowing" it's the right thing for your highest good.

A good test as to whether the voice you're hearing is coming from your Inner Source or not is this: If what you hear takes you away from unconditional love, a deep sense of peace, contentment, inner joy, and a sense of freedom (for you and others), then it's not your Inner Voice. It's a voice from your shell.

There are multiple ways you can cultivate your ability to hear this Inner Voice:

- First, you can purposefully create the conditions conducive for hearing. This is one of the reasons for the daily practice of structured meditation, especially in the morning. Meditation creates a still, silent space where this hearing is possible; otherwise, it's difficult to hear in the incessant chatter of your mind or in the noise of the day. I sometimes refer to this period during my day as "Allowing Inner Guidance" or "Allowing Infinite Intelligence."

- Second, you can pose powerful, open-ended questions before meditation and wait for an answer. In doing this, it's important to not expect an answer immediately. We, as humans, want an answer right now and, typically, search our minds for one. If we don't get an answer right away, we assume we don't know and stop searching. Rather than doing this, you need to ask the question and then leave it open until an answer comes to you whenever and however it arrives. In this way, you're leaving it up to your Inner Source to bring you the answer; you tap into a source infinitely more vast, powerful, and intelligent than your limited mind. You also open yourself up to unlimited possibilities.

- Third, it may come out of the blue as clear and powerful guidance; you have a "knowing" in that moment that it's the right action to take. This becomes more common as you continue down the path of I-Lignment. Learn to trust and take action on this spontaneous "knowing."

Once you let go of fear and learn to always hear, trust, and follow this voice, you'll be empowered in ways you would never have imagined possible! You're no longer dependent on guidance from the outside; your guidance is inside-out!

YOU'VE DISCOVERED THE "SPRING OF LIFE"

When you reach the end of the inward journey, you've discovered your authentic "I." The heartbeat of "I" is your Inner Source. When you're at "I," you're in presence with this Inner Source and will be able to clearly hear its guidance. This is the spring of your Greatest Life!

Now you're ready to create your life masterpiece . . .

PART THREE:

LIVING A LIFE OF PURPOSE, POWER, AND POSSIBILITY

CHAPTER NINE:
LIVING YOUR GREATEST LIFE...
FROM "I"

LET'S RECAP WHERE YOU ARE AT THIS POINT IN I-LIGNMENT...
When you uncover and are living now from your "I"ntersection, from your true "I," the foundation of your new emerging life will be these states of being:

- Unconditional love and deep peace . . . natural states when you're in presence with your Inner Source.
- True freedom . . . a condition that exists at your "I"ntersection, a point in space with infinite degrees of freedom, lived in each new present moment.

- Contentment . . . that exists because you know this is exactly where you need to be and nowhere else.
- Joy . . . that results for no other reason than being in the first three states of being.

All of this is independent of anything else going on around you. It's where you'll discover the stability and deep sense of well-being you've been looking for . . . regardless of the type of life you've lived so far or of the life you'll create in this next part of I-Lignment.

You're also at the point where all things are possible. You've gone from "impossible" in terms of living your Greatest Life when you first started I-Lignment and were still buried in your shell, to discovering *"I" AM possible* once you got closer to the end of your inward journey to "I"; and finally to unlimited possibilities once you were tapped into and trusting the guidance from your Inner Source.

Impossible —> "I" AM Possible —> Unlimited Possibilities

You've now uncovered a beautiful, light-filled clearing in a thick, dark forest. In the middle of the clearing is a crystal-clear, life-giving spring, and surrounding the spring is a well-engineered foundation.

From this inner spring and foundation, you have a solid base and resources to create and live your Greatest Life inside-out . . . an incredible life of purpose, possibility, and passion!

Before you continue on your I-Lignment journey to create your Greatest Life, there are four empowering perspectives that need to be covered first.

"I"NDIVIDUAL FREEDOM

We live in a world where it seems everyone is trying to control everyone else for their own purposes. Many in powerful positions understand the techniques of manipulation and control. They're taking advantage of the majority of us who have developed an outside-in life and, as a result, have develop many underlying emotions, beliefs, and stories that can be easily triggered and produce predictable reactions. As long as this continues, you're not living life; life is living you. You're living an inauthentic life in constant reaction to the people and events around you. You're being controlled. You need to break free!

You've taken the first huge steps to do this by bringing yourself out of your time-based shell to your "I"ntersection, and then by tapping into your Inner Guidance. You've released the emotional triggers and stopped relying on guidance only from others. At this point, true individual freedom becomes possible. Without this freedom, your transformation to your Greatest Life is impossible.

As you begin to create your Greatest Life, you'll be met with resistance from others as you attempt to change. There's another perspective you must have to stay free and independent through complete transformation.

SELFISH CREATION . . . SELFLESS EXECUTION

Most of us have been caught in the dilemma between being focused on ourselves or being focused on others. If we began focusing only on ourselves during periods of our life, we were told we were being selfish and needed to unselfishly focus only on others. Many times, this was said by a person or persons who wanted us to focus on them for their benefit or perhaps wanted to control us. If we submitted to the pressure, we took our attention off ourselves and gave it once again to others. We became part of their agenda . . . their plans and goals . . . not ours. We, in essence, gave up our individual freedom to others' demands and reinforced our outside-in way of life. This happens all the time in marriages, extended families, friendships, social groups, workplaces, and politics.

People make it an either/or judgment: we're either seen as being selfish or unselfish. In reality, you need to have the ability to use either one or the other at the appropriate times. When you're going on your inward journey during I-Lignment, you need to do it by yourself, for yourself only. This is a selfish time. The same applies when you're determining your Greatest Life defined by your Inner Purpose, Dynamic Possibility, and Intentions. All of this must come from within you if it's to be authentic. This, too, is a selfish time. By being selfish during both these times, you maintain your independence and freedom.

This doesn't mean you can't still be engaged in your daily life, as you're going through your transformation, in a kind, giving way; it's the process of transformation that you keep private and do only for yourself. But then you become radically unselfish (selfless) as you take your Greatest Life to the world to serve others, bringing tremendous value to their lives.

Bottom line: Use both selfishness and selflessness as tools on your transformational journey and allow others to do the same. In the end, everyone benefits.

TRUE CREATIVITY

True creativity comes from within; anything else is copying. If you study true geniuses and innovators, they were inspired by something inside them. So often their great inventions or new ideas intuitively came to them out of the blue. Many times, they were fiercely resisted by popular wisdom and thinking, yet the truth and power of their original innovation prevailed.

The same applies to you. If you try to get inspiration for the creation of your Greatest Life while living in and from your shell, the creation will be sourced from the past or current input of others. Anything you create will be limited to what input is available through them and will potentially contain the same dysfunctional and self-limiting attributes.

By being connected to your Inner Source, you're tapped into a true creative reservoir of unlimited possibilities, infinite wisdom, endless resources, and empowering energy. Any creative endeavor becomes possible . . . without limitation. You're, in effect, co-creating life from within.

CREATIVE DIRECTOR OF YOUR LIFE

I've always loved the title "creative director" in a digital marketing company. A creative director determines the creative vision of a project and manifests that vision through digital technology. They create the vision and then pull resources together from many disciplines to make it a reality.

Be the creative director of your life! Start with a blank sheet and let your creative juices flow!

Now is the opportunity to start your new creative project . . . your Greatest Life!

Let's see how . . .

There are six essential steps to this part of your I-Lignment journey:

- Be in the "Flow" . . . from Within
- Uncovering Your Life's Purpose
- Dynamic Possibility
- Intentions
- I-Ligned Life . . . in Each Moment
- Authentic Connection with Others

Let's discuss each of these now . . .

BE IN THE "FLOW" . . . FROM WITHIN

The phrase "just flow with life" is one that I've felt uncomfortable with most of my life. I couldn't figure out why I felt that way. It sounded like a good idea, but it also felt, in a way, like giving up control over my own life. It wasn't until much later, after I started working on I-Lignment, that I discovered why I resisted "getting into the flow."

The way most people use the phrase, they imply you need to get in the flow of life happening around you; to live your life in the flow of your life circumstances. Much of this outside "flow" is caused by the other people around you, in addition to yourself, all living in and from your respective shells. By this time, you know what that means: a polluted river of dysfunction. As proof, either turn on the TV and watch the news or look at the inner workings of your own extended family. In effect, you see one person's dysfunctional shell clashing up against another person's dysfunctional shell. Why would you want to "just flow" with that life? Being in the "outside flow of life" is living a life outside-in; you're allowing other outside forces to dictate your life.

I finally realized it isn't life outside of us we need to get in the flow of; it's the flow from within, from our Inner Source. Once you tap into that source and find a way to turn on the spigot, it will flow through you and out of you into the world; you'll be flowing your life from an infinite repository of deep peace, unconditional love, intelligence, resources, creativity, and possibilities . . . through the Inner Guidance you "hear."

From this Inner Source will flow your life purpose and Dynamic Possibility. Once you know how you're going to powerfully engage in and contribute to the world, you can then get into the outside flow of life in a way that is meaningful, powerful, and impactful. Based on your purpose and possibility, you can place yourself in that outer flow in a way that brings the highest good to others. You decide how you engage in the world, who and what you engage with, and who and what you ignore . . . rather than just "being in that flow." Your life becomes a life on purpose . . . inside-out.

ALLOWING INFINITE INTELLIGENCE

You tap into this inner flow of life by always hearing, trusting, and following your Inner Voice. It allows you to create and then live your life inside-out. As you follow the guidance of your Inner Voice, the people and resources you need to do what is asked of you will flow into your life, as if by magic, at the right time and place. You'll be living in a world of abundance.

FLOW . . . FROM LOVE

Remember, one of the core truths of life mentioned earlier is, "We are all looking for one thing in life . . . unconditional love." You've brought yourself to your "I"ntersection and made the connection to your Inner Source. In doing so, you've tapped into an infinite supply of unconditional love and have now become it. You ARE unconditional love. As you get into the flow from within, you can radiate that love through you and out into the world in all directions indiscriminately.

As you develop your new life inside-out, make unconditional love the undercurrent of everything you do. Flow it into the creation of your purpose and Dynamic Possibility. Flow it into the way you feel, think, speak, and act. Flow it into the lives of others. Flow it into the value you bring to the world.

By doing so, you'll have a transformative impact on your own life, the lives of others, and the world around you. Unconditional love, one of the highest levels of conscious energy, has the power to dissolve all the other lower levels of unconscious energy (hate, fear, guilt, regret). Many luminaries have shown how this is possible: Martin Luther King Jr., Jesus, Dalai Lama, Buddha, Mother Teresa, Mahatma Gandhi, my grandmother Ester . . . to name just a few.

Out of this Inner Flow will emerge one thing that will bring you into alignment with your Greatest Life . . .

UNCOVERING YOUR LIFE'S PURPOSE

An angelic, older woman showed up in my life at a coffee shop many years ago as I sat struggling over a difficult personal issue. When I first saw her, I immediately felt her aura of love, peacefulness, and calmness even as she stood in line thirty feet away. She got her coffee and made her way to the table next to mine. She looked a bit disheveled. I thought she might be homeless, but her demeanor contradicted that judgment. She smiled brightly and started talking to me immediately. I think she sensed I needed someone to talk to.

Over the next hour, she shared many words of wisdom that were perfect to help me get unstuck and out of my slump. It was amazing how each piece of perspective and advice was perfect for my situation. Then, with much reluctance and prodding from me, she began to tell me her life story. She had been, four years before, a successful businesswoman at the top of her life. Then the diagnosis of a serious cancer came. She had to stop working as she went through four years of difficult, costly treatments with limited and diminishing success. She had to sell off all her assets and had become penniless, living out of her car for the past two years.

It was a tragic story, yet she glowed the entire time we talked, even though she had less than a year to live. She told me she had made a commitment, when she became homeless, that it would not define who she was nor how she showed up in life. In the midst of all her struggles, she discovered her true calling for the remainder of her life!

Her purpose every day was to show up in public spaces

and find that one person who needed her help to get beyond a personal struggle. Her life purpose turned her from being weak and afraid into a powerhouse of a person focused every day on transforming someone else's life. I offered some money for all she had done for me in those couple of hours, but she refused. I felt so blessed to have had her come into my life!

WHAT IS MY PURPOSE IN LIFE?

How many times have you asked this question? You've asked this because you've probably been living a life that feels empty, unfulfilled, and lacking clear direction. You know intuitively that what you're trying to accomplish isn't your true calling, but you don't know what is. You have a nagging feeling that you could be living a much more meaningful life . . . one that brings so much more to your life, to the lives of those you care about, and to the world in general.

Until now, you've been disconnected from your authentic self, getting conflicting, disjointed guidance for your direction from others; you were blinded by the demands and influence of the many voices around you. If you came up with a purpose, it was most likely coming from this outside-in source; it was limiting and kept you stuck on a linear, time-based path. It didn't feel authentic . . . and it most likely wasn't!

The Powerful Question from "I." But now you have discovered your authentic "I" . . . are connected to your Inner Source of Life . . . are flowing your life from within . . . and are listening to your Inner Voice for guidance. You're now uniquely positioned to hear your True Purpose, a gift you're destined to bring to the world.

Simply ask the open-ended question, "What is my life

purpose?" at the beginning of your daily meditations. Then deeply listen and allow the answer to come to you. If it doesn't come right away, keep asking until it does; and it will at the right time and place. It's inevitable.

When your purpose comes from the freedom of your "I"ntersection, it's coming from a place of no limitations . . . only infinite possibilities. It comes from the inside-out without the constraints of the remembered past or restricted future. Only from here can you hear your highest calling.

It's important to understand that your True Purpose may remain the same throughout your life, or, since it's coming from a source of infinite possibilities, it may evolve to an even higher calling.

As I went through my own personal transformation, I posed the question during each meditation, "What is my purpose?" Eventually it emerged and was extremely clear:

"I help people realize their Greatest Life . . . to Be Free—Live Free—Work Free."

As soon as I discovered it, my life coalesced around and became aligned with that purpose. Things I needed to make the purpose a reality began to be attracted into my life naturally.

Underlying True Purpose. When you discover your True Purpose in this way, it will naturally be imbued with the attributes of "I" . . . unconditional love, peacefulness, and true freedom. You'll also naturally flow these out into the world as you live your purpose. If you don't feel it has these attributes in the service of others, it isn't your True Purpose. If it's not, keep searching until you find the one that does.

True Purpose Is Timeless . . . Just Be It. There is no time in purpose; it's timeless. When you discover your purpose, become it right now . . . in this present moment. Making money at your life's purpose isn't a prerequisite for becoming it. As soon as you decide it's your purpose, then be it in that instant. Then continue to get Inner Guidance daily, allowing your purpose to emerge and evolve in a form that will deliver the greatest good to you and others . . . in the form of a Dynamic Possibility (discussed in the next section).

Think about a flower. A flower doesn't try to be anything other than what it is, nor does it compare itself to anything else. It simply knows its purpose. It takes root, grows, blooms, and then sits there looking and smelling beautiful . . . bringing that beauty into the lives all around it. Once you find your purpose, become it immediately and then allow it to bloom into the world from within.

Being of service to others. As mentioned earlier in this chapter, you discover your authentic purpose "selfishly"; you'll never find it in collaboration with others. It's a discovery that you alone make from within . . . by asking the question "What is my purpose?" and listening for the answer in silence.

Once you find it, though, you then bring your purpose to the world powerfully in the service of others. You become dedicated to something much greater than just yourself. Living your purpose in the service of others is the only way to realize your Greatest Life. Just like the woman in the coffee shop, you'll then live large and strong rather than small and weak . . . as you share your gift.

Now bring your purpose to life through a . . .

DYNAMIC POSSIBILITY

*"Go confidently in the direction of your dreams!
Live the life you've imagined!"*
—HENRY DAVID THOREAU

Orville and Wilbur Wright believed in the possibility of flight, the ability of a heavier-than-air machine to stay aloft indefinitely. Even though their belief in air flight was highly doubted at the time, they persisted in their research and innovation until proving their theory with the now famous fifty-nine-second powered, sustained, and controlled bi-wing airplane flight at Kitty Hawk, North Carolina, in 1903. Two years later they built and flew the first practical airplane.

Creating from the foundation established by the Wright brothers, others envisioned and brought to reality new aviation possibilities in the ensuing years. Sixty-six years later, the first person landed on the moon!

Anything is possible! The seemingly impossible *is* possible! Don't dream small . . . dream big!

YOUR DYNAMIC POSSIBILITY

Having gone through I-Lignment to this point, you now have a new clearing in your life . . . a newfound freedom at "I," an Inner Purpose, and endless possibilities. You have a new life that is no longer defined by the past or constrained by the future . . . nor controlled by others. This is the pivotal moment where you can create and live your Greatest Life!

Just like the Wright brothers, you have a possibility you're destined to bring to the world in this moment. What is it?

Once you discover it, you can plop it right in the middle of your "clearing" and start living it now. Your life can pivot in a whole new direction . . . instantaneously.

DISCOVERING YOUR POSSIBILITY

Your Dynamic Possibility is anything you can envision that is in alignment with your life's purpose and will allow you to live your Greatest Life, in service of others, while living in and from your authentic "I." It's a bold vision on how you want to show up in life and make a powerful difference! When realized, this possibility will cause you to jump out of bed, ready for the day to begin, so you can engage with the people you've chosen to serve!

When envisioning your possibility . . .

Be Bold!

Be Unlimited!

Be Wild with Creating the New You!

Be Your Dream!

Be Your Destiny!

Choose an amazing possibility that ignites your passions!

While creating your possibility, you can ask yourself questions such as . . .

- What type of life would cause me to wake every morning with passion, ready to jump out of bed to serve others?

- What type of life could I be living that would make retiring a foolish concept?
- Whom do I want to serve?
- What type of life could I live that would make the biggest positive difference to those I love and want to serve?
- What type of life would bring the most joy to me and those I love?
- What does my Greatest Life look like?

Your possibility can be expansive and worldwide, or it can be simple and close to home. It doesn't matter which as long as it inspires *you* and allows *you* to fulfill your purpose and live your greatest gift in service of others!

As an example, my Dynamic Possibility is shown in Appendix D.

A simpler Dynamic Possibility is from one of my clients:

*"Being a Leader Creating Solutions
to Transform Homelessness."*

*"Creator of a Loving Home Environment . . .
Empowering Myself, My Life Partner, My Sons, My
Extended Family, and My Friends to Live Loving,
Inspired, and Successful Lives."*

When you create your possibility, put it in present tense rather than in future tense. This is important, as you know by now! If you put it in future tense, it's always going to happen sometime in the future, a future that never arrives nor exists. The possibility is weakened. If you put it in present tense, it's a reality now; you become it in the only time you have to make it happen. The possibility becomes powerful.

BE OPEN TO AN EVEN GREATER POSSIBILITY

The adjective "dynamic" in Dynamic Possibility was used specifically because your possibility may and most likely will change; you need to stay open to have it evolve to even more powerful possibilities. It may evolve through three forms as you go through your I-Lignment transformation.

"Possibility" . . . without Knowing Your Life Purpose

You don't want to wait until you reach your authentic "I" and discover your True Purpose before living your life. If you aren't currently living in a way that inspires you and is of service to others, then create a possibility that will allow you to do so. While you're waiting to discover your True Purpose, you'll thus be engaged in the world and contributing to the lives of others through your chosen possibility.

"Possibility" . . . Flowing from Your Life Purpose

Once you uncover your life's purpose, you can go through the process of discovering all the potential possibilities that are in alignment with your purpose. Then you can pick the one that gets you most inspired and brings the greatest good to those you want to serve.

"Higher Possibility" . . . Attracted to You from Your Intentions

As you pursue all your intentions (discussed in the next section), they have the power to attract an even more powerful possibility into your life. It's important to keep yourself open and aware to one showing up when you least expect it. By doing so, you may end up living a possibility that is far beyond your wildest dreams!

CREATING YOUR I-LIGNED LIFE PLAN

As creative director of your life, it's time to design your I-Ligned Life Plan, which brings your life's purpose and Dynamic Possibility to realization . . . created from the inside-out . . . from your authentic "I."

There are six key elements to creating this plan. We've discussed the first two:

- #1: Your Life's Purpose
- #2: Dynamic Possibility

Now the question is, How are you going to take both into the world to serve others? This is where the last four elements of your plan come into play.

- #3: People You're Here to Serve (including Yourself)
- #4: Areas of Attention . . . in Your Life
- #5: Goals (for Each Area of Attention)
- #6: Strategies (to Realize the Goals) and Actions (to Accomplish Each Strategy)

Let's talk about the remaining elements of the plan you will be creating.

#3: PEOPLE YOU'RE HERE TO SERVE (Including Yourself)

It would be nice if you could serve everyone in the world and bring incredible value into all their lives, but that sounds exhausting; you just might be spread too thin and not serve anyone well. You need to look at your purpose and Dynamic Possibility and then decide who (what groups of people) you would like to serve that would receive the greatest benefit.

#4: AREAS OF ATTENTION . . . IN YOUR LIFE

It's important you look at all areas of your life holistically as you decide where to place your attention. People tend to focus on just one part of their lives as they develop life plans. If they do, it usually leads to imbalance and unhappiness. Common examples of this are an intense, singular focus on work or a complete devotion to spouse, kids, and family. With a singular focus, other parts of their lives suffer. Also, if a disaster happens in that one part of life (for example, being fired from a job or getting a divorce), then the person is devastated; it feels as if their life has ended . . . and, in many respects, it has.

#5: GOALS (For each Area of Attention)

For each area of attention, you now determine what you want to achieve (goals) in the service of others in that group. You can have multiple goals in the same area. When you create the goal, make sure you include a way to measure when you have attained it.

#6: STRATEGIES (To Realize the Goals) AND ACTIONS (To Accomplish Each Strategy)

For each goal, you now determine the strategies for accomplishing that goal and the actions required to achieve the strategies.

To get your creative juices flowing, here's a partial example of an I-Ligned Life Plan:

I-LIGNED LIFE PLAN EXAMPLE

PURPOSE

"I'm Changing the World through Music . . . Creating Greater Unity and Love between People"

DYNAMIC POSSIBILITY

"I AM a master and well-known recording artist with my own state-of-the-art recording studio . . . serving artists creating music to promote love and unity. I coach other musicians on how to create, record, and perform music in a way that transforms lives. I'm powerfully connected with music professionals around the world collaborating to make a powerful difference. I travel extensively throughout the world, bringing music into the lives of those who have recently gone through a difficult time. My life is filled with amazing experiences and adventures."

PEOPLE BEING SERVED

- Musicians Wanting to Transform Lives
- Children Impacted by Natural Disasters
- My Parents
- My Friends
- Myself

AREAS OF ATTENTION ... IN MY LIFE

- Professional Artist and Music Coach ... supporting Musicians Wanting to Transform Lives.
- Recording Studio Professional . . . Recording Music for Musicians Wanting to Transform Lives.
- Contribution . . . Bringing Comfort to Children Impacted by Disaster through Music
- Spiritual Leader . . . Bringing Deep Meaning into People's Lives through Music.
- Adventurer and Explorer
- Daughter
- Friend

Now taking two of the areas of attention as examples to show the goals, strategies, and actions . . .

PROFESSIONAL ARTIST AND MUSIC COACH ... SUPPORTING MUSICIANS WANTING TO TRANSFORM LIVES (AREA OF ATTENTION)

- Goal: Innovate five music events with other artists to create unity between conflicted groups . . . to enable them to see the oneness between all people through music. Complete by December 31.
  - Strategy: Create a concert series in Chicago with a powerful and uplifting theme of unity.
    - Action: Set up planning session for first concert in Chicago on April 9th.
    - Action: Contact local, influential musician in Chicago to partner with to bring together other musicians for the event.

> ## DAUGHTER (AREA OF ATTENTION)
> - Goal: Love and support my parents by staying open and maintaining strong and deep connections through twenty-four planned get-togethers each year.
>   - Strategy: Take them out for coffee every month.
>   - Action: Take them for coffee at the Stimulus Coffee & Bakery House on Jan 5.
>   - Strategy: Get them out into nature every other month.
>   - Action: Take them on a nature hike along the Clackamas River in the Clackamas River Canyon Wilderness Area next Wednesday.

TRUST IN INFINITE RESOURCES

I've been doing strategic planning all my life, both for business as well as personally. One of the biggest inhibitors to creating a powerful plan is the planner's perception of a lack of resources to accomplish what they envision. If they don't think they have enough time, people, and money to do something, they leave it off the plan or don't even bring it up. The plan ends up being much less grand than it could be or it's incomplete, not whole. You can't live your Greatest Life if your life plan isn't big, bold, and powerful . . . extending well beyond what you think you're capable of doing on your own and with your perceived limited resources.

That's why, as you go through the process of developing your I-Ligned Life Plan, don't think about where the time and resources (opportunities, people, money, materials) are coming from until the end of the planning process. Only then do you circle back and determine who is going to complete each action, when the actions will be completed, and where the resources are coming from. If you don't know, then put TBD (to be determined) and trust they will arrive at the right time and place.

There are infinite resources all around you; we live in a world of abundance. Just because you don't see them or know how to access them doesn't mean they don't exist. If you develop a powerful plan and make it visible to the world around you, the resources will be naturally drawn to your plan. They'll begin to arrive in unexpected ways and from unexpected people. If you keep yourself open to all possibilities, stay present, and become infinitely resourceful, you'll find them.

Now to open your life to even greater possibilities . . .

INTENTIONS

"I"ntention: a thing intended; an aim . . . flowing from your authentic "I" (new definition).

When living in and from your shell, your intentions were anything but focused; they didn't have a clear, authentic purpose. Many times, they were disempowering and led you away from your best life. They reflected the chaotic, dysfunctional makeup of your shell as their source.

Now you're making a powerful shift to new "I"ntentions flowing from your Inner Source . . . that will transform your past limited life to your Greatest Life!

To make this shift, you need to stay open and tapped into this source of infinite possibilities and its boundless opportunities and resources in the world around you . . . allowing them to be attracted into your life. You do this by getting clear and focused on your four "I"ntentions.

- "I"ntention 1: Your Life's Purpose
- "I"ntention 2: Your Dynamic Possibility and I-Ligned Life Plan
- "I"ntention 3: "I" FEEL . . .
- "I"ntention 4: "I" AM . . .

YOUR LIFE'S PURPOSE

When you discovered your life's purpose, it gave you a compass setting, your true north. You knew which path to start heading down, of all the possible paths. But then you needed to determine what to do as you traveled down the path that would make the journey spectacular and valuable for you and others. The "what" possibilities that were in alignment with your purpose began to be attracted into your awareness.

YOUR DYNAMIC POSSIBILITY AND I-LIGNED LIFE PLAN

Of all the possibilities that came to you, there was one that was ideal for this moment. Once you uncovered it, it became an organizing focal point; you built a plan around that possibility to bring it to realization. The result: your I-Ligned Life Plan. It's specific and actionable. It's how you want to intentionally live your life and be of value to others in the world.

While you're allowing this purpose-driven Dynamic Possibility to unfold in your life, however, you need to keep yourself open for better ways for it to happen different from how it's already defined in your I-Ligned Life Plan. You also need to keep yourself open for even greater possibilities.

There are two ways of doing this.

"I" FEEL AND "I" AM . . . NAVIGATION TOOLS FOR EMPOWERING YOUR JOURNEY

Once you have created your possibility, it's important to discover two things that attracted you to it. The first is how you're "feeling" while living in and from the possibility, expressed as "I" FEEL _____. The second is how you're "being" while living in and from the possibility, expressed as "I" AM _____.

Both are what you want to experience in life. "I" FEEL _____ will make it clear how you want to feel in your new life; "I" AM _____ will make it clear how you want to show up in your new life.

Both are powerful on your life journey in multiple ways.

First, they become navigation tools as you further develop and then live your possibility. You can refer to each list as you make decisions. You can ask yourself, "Does the decision allow me to experience them more fully . . . or does it diminish them?"

Second, you can use them to evaluate what you're feeling, thinking, saying, and doing in that moment. If what you are feeling, thinking, saying, and doing aren't in alignment with how you want to feel or how you want to show up in life, then you're clearly aware of it and can choose to do things differently.

Third, they can be used to evaluate other possibilities. Ask yourself, "Does the new possibility allow me to better experience them than my existing possibility?" If it does, you can seriously consider switching to the new possibility to live an even greater life.

To give you an idea what they might look like, below are typical examples:

"I" FEEL

- I FEEL . . . a loving, close relationship with God!
- I FEEL . . . authentic!
- I FEEL . . . love!
- I FEEL . . . free!
- I FEEL . . . connected!
- I FEEL . . . whole!
- I FEEL . . . peaceful!
- I FEEL . . . that I'm in the flow of life . . . from within!
- I FEEL . . . content!
- I FEEL . . . kind!
- I FEEL . . . excited!
- I FEEL . . . joyful!
- I FEEL . . . I contribute to many people's success!
- I FEEL . . . successful!
- I FEEL . . . accomplished!
- I FEEL . . . abundant . . . in all aspects of my life!
- I FEEL . . . physically strong, healthy, and flexible!

When you discover the feelings you want in your life, they'll put the power of positive emotions behind *any* possibility you choose. These high-energy emotions will bring your possibility to life.

Interestingly (but not surprising), you'll find the desired feelings most people have in common while in their possibility are those feelings inherent at "I": love, peace, freedom, and joy.

"I" AM

- "I" AM . . . living in simplicity, freedom, and unlimited possibility.
- "I" AM . . . living life now . . . in this present moment.
- "I" AM . . . living from "I" . . . being unconditional love, deep peace, contentment, and radiant joy.
- "I" AM . . . following my Inner Source . . . being in the flow of life from the inside-out.
- "I" AM . . . a powerful entrepreneur bringing innovative solutions in service of others.
- "I" AM . . . being abundant in all parts of my life.
- "I" AM . . . an athlete-in-training.
- "I" AM . . . being radiant well-being . . . energetic, strong, healthy, flexible, and relaxed.
- "I" AM . . . creating a mobile, virtual life, allowing me to be where I can best serve others.
- "I" AM . . . an investor in real estate.
- "I" AM . . . living a life of adventure and many experiences.
- "I" AM . . . attracting people into my life who empower my journey.
- "I" AM . . . being with my life partner . . . bringing

unconditional love, peace, contentment, and adventure into her life.

- "I" AM . . . being a loving father and friend to my sons and daughters.
- "I" AM . . . being a loving friend to my core group of friends and extended family.
- "I" AM . . . bringing love, listening, understanding, compassion, and forgiveness into all my relationships.
- "I" AM . . . a spark for others' success.
- "I" AM . . . being financially independent . . . positioned to pursue my purpose and possibilities.

By developing your list of "I" AM thoughts and repeating them to yourself regularly, you replace your limiting "i" am (small "i") thoughts of who you are (for example, "i" am not good enough, "i" am not loved, "i" am weak, "i" am abandoned) with empowering thoughts representing who you are in truth . . . living powerfully in and from your authentic "I." This is what puts power behind and reinforces your new possibility! You're re-creating who you "think" you are . . . and your new "I" AM will show up in your life instead!

POWERFUL MAGNETISM

What you attract into your life is in direct proportion to what you're putting into the world.

There's a coffee shop experiment you need to try sometime that demonstrates this. One day when you're feeling down and negative, go into a crowded coffee shop and observe the body language of the people around you. They'll feel your negative, chaotic energy and literally move and look away from you to escape your energy's impact on them. On another day, when your life is going great and you're feeling upbeat, go into the same coffee shop when it's crowded and observe other people's body language once again. You'll find they move toward you, make eye contact, and, in many cases, engage in conversation. They're attracted to your energy and want more of it.

This is the principle of magnetism. The motion of electrically charged particles found in all matter gives off electric currents that create a magnetic field; it creates magnetism. Your intentions are no different. They create a field of energy that extends well beyond you that naturally attracts things to them or repels things. If you examine your life, you'll find many examples of this magnetism at work.

At this point in your transformation, you've made the third Shift of Transformation: the Shift of Intention. You're projecting powerful, positive, emotionally charged intentions. The combination of these four intentions creates a powerful magnetism that will begin to attract things to you, many times in unexpected ways, that will bring your possibility to life. You, in essence, have asked the abundant Universe to conspire to help you . . . and it will! As your intentions are fulfilled, you'll be living your Greatest Life!

However, to realize your Greatest Life, you need to live an . . .

I-LIGNED LIFE . . . IN EACH MOMENT

I grew up spending a lot of time in the Willamette Valley, a fertile area in Oregon filled with fields, vineyards, and orchards of fruits, vegetables, hops, and flowers. I developed a love and appreciation of farmers and their way of life, especially small, family-run farms with less sophisticated equipment. They're salt-of-the-earth people. They have their hands in the soil with an intimate connection with the growing process. They deeply understand the importance of creating the right conditions before planting the seed and the need to nurture the plant at each step of its growth for it to flourish.

Your "seeds" are your intentions; the "field" in which you need to create the "right conditions" for those seeds to grow and flourish is each new present moment. You need to create the fertile soil that will allow an I-Ligned life to emerge . . . your life lived in and from your authentic "I" . . . following your Inner Guidance . . . leading to your Greatest Life.

These right conditions are the daily practice of Empowering the "I"ntersection.

EMPOWERING THE "I"NTERSECTION

Farmers develop a routine that is consistent yet open and flexible, allowing for changing conditions. It's based on a combination of science, process, the right tools, and intuition, taking the right actions in each moment. They have a razor-sharp focus on the growing process in the moment, lest they lose their whole crop.

Anyone who has mastered anything knows how important

a routine is. You need to do the same for your life. An Empowering the "I"ntersection daily routine allows you to systematically, yet naturally and intuitively, go through the process of I-Lignment.

As you know, there are Four Shifts of Transformation: the Shift of Perspective, the Shift of Source, the Shift of Intention, and the Shift of Attention. The first three shifts were discussed earlier in the book. The fourth shift, the Shift of Attention, is made real through this routine. It allows the shift to occur while you're living your everyday life; you bring your attention every day to those things most important to your transformation and to the realization of your Greatest Life.

Below are the main elements of this routine.

Empowering the "I"ntersection . . . Daily Routine

Morning

- Wake Up in Gratitude.
- Review Intentions (Purpose, Dynamic Possibility, "I" FEEL, "I" AM).
- Meditate and Release.
- Meditate and Listen for Inner Guidance.
- Create "Plan for the Day" based on your I-Ligned Life Plan and Inner Guidance.

During Day

- Execute "Plan for the Day."
- Be Aware of and Open to Opportunities Showing Up.

- Meditate on the Fly . . . to Release Blocks and Receive Guidance in the Moment.
- Peak Energy and Wellness Routine.

Evening

- Meditate and Release before Bed.
- Ask Powerful Open-Ended Questions.
- Meditate and Release If You Wake Up during Sleep with Emotional or Mental Stress.

NOTE: There are many ways to do anything. The order of this list can be rearranged to fit your specific style and way of living. However, you should try to use it in this specific order, if possible; it was created this way intentionally for maximum impact.

As you use the routine through the process of I-Lignment, its use and emphasis will change along the way. At first, it'll be used to empower you as you journey inward to your "I"ntersection . . . your authentic "I." Then it will shift to empower you to create a life from the inside-out . . . uncovering your innermost intentions. Last, it will become a way of life, in each moment, as you bring your intentions to reality.

Let's see how this daily practice is creating the conditions for your Greatest Life to unfold . . .

YOU'RE IN GRATITUDE ... IN THE MOMENT!

Waking up being grateful for another beautiful moment in your life is a powerful way to start your day. You're grateful not only for another day to enjoy but for all that life will be bringing you as part of the unfolding of your Greatest Life.

By being grateful, you see everything during the day as an opportunity. You see the opportunity for taking action on your I-Ligned Life Plan. You also see an opportunity in everything that comes your way during the day: an opportunity to accept if it moves you toward or empowers your intentions; an opportunity to ignore if it moves you away from or disempowers your intentions; or an opportunity to accept an event or person as a trigger that is pointing you to an emotion or inhibiting belief that needs to be seen, heard, and ultimately released to dissolve your shell . . . which also ultimately empowers your intentions.

Most important, you feel gratitude for all the opportunities to serve others and bring value into their lives.

Your "Attention" . . . Is on Being Grateful for Everything in Your Life!

YOU'RE PRESENT ... IN THE MOMENT!

By meditating in the morning, evening, and throughout the day, you're increasing your experience of being present. You're having more experience being in the only time that is real . . . each new present moment. You're living an increasingly real life.

You're also spending more time in the place where all your power exists to do anything . . . now. Your ability to get things done will increase exponentially.

By being present *internally* through daily meditation, you're also connected to and are able to receive guidance from your Inner Source. You're focused on receiving that guidance in the morning to help create your "plan for the day" but also throughout the day as you release and connect internally on the fly.

By being present *externally*, you're experiencing life every day as it is in reality, not distorted by the past or future. You're better able to see beyond the surface of life in front of you and connect with all around you at a much deeper level. You're also much more aware when opportunities come to you to help fulfill your intentions.

By being present, you're at your "I"ntersection (if only for a short time at the beginning of the I-Lignment process), which has the inherent states of unconditional love, deep peace, and true freedom. You're able to fill your love bucket daily from an unlimited source and share it freely with others.

As you continue the practice of being present daily, it will ultimately become a way of life and can be experienced in each and every moment.

Your "Attention" . . . Is on Being Present!

YOU'RE RELEASING TO STAY PRESENT . . . IN THE MOMENT!

Throughout I-Lignment, you need to be vigilant at clearing out the weeds that will choke out the emerging plants in the field. Without this constant releasing of your inhibiting emotions and beliefs, your seeds of intentions will never emerge nor be fulfilled; they'll be choked off by the smothering debris of your shell.

When you commit to dedicated periods of time in the morning and evening to meditate and then release, you give yourself focused periods to feel yourself being triggered, feel the inhibiting emotions and beliefs, hear the message, and then release them. You are, in effect, chipping away at your shell, your inauthentic small "i" . . . decreasing its influence over and impact on your life. You're continuing to cultivate a clear field for your "I"ntentions to grow in. This is reinforced by meditating and releasing on the fly throughout the day when you feel yourself being triggered.

As you continue this daily practice, the dedicated periods in the morning/evening and the on-the-fly moments will merge; the daily practice of meditate and release will transform into a way of life. You'll become adept at feeling the emotion and belief, hearing the message, and then releasing on the fly in each moment.

This constant releasing is critical to allow you to naturally and powerfully "Be in the Flow . . . from Within" as well as engage, with "I"ntention, in the external flow of the world around you . . . without getting stuck or blocked by the past or future. In effect, you get to the point where you die and start anew in each moment, focused only on the unfolding of your "I"ntentions in that present moment.

Your "Attention" . . . Is on Removing Anything That Inhibits Living Life Now!

YOU'RE FOLLOWING INNER GUIDANCE . . . IN THE MOMENT!

"The heart can think of no devotion, greater than being shore to ocean. Holding the curve of one position, counting an endless repetition."
—ROBERT FROST

Through meditation, you bring yourself present, quiet your mind, enter a silent space, and then listen for Inner Guidance. By consistently listening and trusting that guidance, you are the shore for the ocean of your Inner Source.

During the morning routine, you first meditate and release on any blocks you feel to being present and in presence. You then meditate and listen for Inner Guidance. The same happens at night but in a slightly different way. You meditate and release on any blocks you feel to being present and in presence. You then pose an open-ended question on something you're needing answers to and then go to sleep, allowing the answer to come to you at the right time . . . perhaps in the middle of the night or the next morning.

As you continue to practice meditating and listening for guidance during these dedicated times and then applying the same to on-the-fly moments, you eventually develop the ability to get quiet and then hear Inner Guidance in any moment. This is when you are in a true flow of life from the inside-out; you hear the guidance, trust it, and then let your life (emotions, thoughts, words, and actions) flow from that guidance . . . always.

There are six blocks to this inside-out flow that are common when trying to trust and follow your Inner Voice, especially as you're going through transformation. You need to watch out for these blocks and release them as they occur. Otherwise, you'll stay stuck, looking for them to be fulfilled in the outside world and continue to live outside-in . . . not hearing or following your Inner Guidance.

Wanting Unconditional Love. As long as you're looking for unconditional love from others, their opinion and approval matters immensely. If you're trying to follow your Inner Guidance, but the guidance you hear will lead to a negative opinion or disapproval from these people and have them "love you less," then you'll have a hard time following your Inner Guidance. You must first release "wanting love" from others with a knowing that it exists in unlimited supply, independent of others, when you're living in and from your "I"ntersection. By doing this, you'll receive more love from others in the long run.

Wanting Peace. Who doesn't want more peace? You look for peace by trying to smooth out the rough edges of your external life; you try to just "get along" with others. This is evidenced by you saying yes when you want to say no or saying no when you want to say yes. It also happens when you just go along with the crowd even though you don't agree. Looking for peace in the external world will make it hard to follow your Inner Guidance when it goes against the grain of others and will create conflict and discord. You need to let go of "wanting peace," knowing the true and deep peace you're looking for already exists when living in and from your "I"ntersection . . . independent of life circumstances and other people.

Wanting Freedom. The desire for personal freedom is strong. You search for it out in the world and look to others to give it to you. As long as you're looking outside of yourself to others for your freedom, you'll never find it. You put yourself in a position to be manipulated by those very people who have "granted" you this freedom; there's always the threat of it being taken away by them at a moment's notice. When you know your freedom can be taken away by others, it's hard to follow your Inner Guidance when that guidance may upset these people. True freedom exists only at your "I"ntersection; it's where you have complete freedom to choose your intentions . . . living a purposeful life of your choosing from within. You need to let go of "wanting freedom," knowing that true freedom already exists when you're living in and from your "I"ntersection.

Wanting Control. When you're living an outside-in life, you're by and large controlled by others. As a result, you feel a lack of control and, therefore, want and seek control over your life and the world around you. This "wanting control" blocks the ability to hear, trust, and then follow your Inner Voice. You want to have control and will resist any guidance, especially if it conflicts with what you had planned on doing. When this happens, you need to first stop and release "wanting control" in that moment and then trust and do what you're being internally guided to do. You can do this because you know you'll have inner control as well as control over how you show up in the world when living in and from your "I"ntersection while following your intentions.

Wanting Approval. When living outside-in, you learn to seek guidance outside of yourself for most of what you do. If you try to follow your Inner Guidance, your natural reaction is to first seek approval from others before doing it, especially if it represents any big change in your life or creates a feeling of fear. This "wanting approval" blocks the ability to trust and then follow your Inner Voice implicitly, especially if the guidance won't get the approval of others. You'll get all the approval you'll need (internal and external) when living from your "I"ntersection.

Wanting Security. Living in and from your shell is a scary, fearful place (in your mind), where you don't feel like you have a lot of stability in your life. You're buffeted around by the constant changes and the multitude of influences over your life, current and past. You seek consistency and certainty; you want security. This stops you from taking action on anything unfamiliar or that you don't understand. It makes trusting and following your Inner Guidance without question difficult if it takes you down an unknown path. You can release "wanting security," knowing true security is achieved by following your Inner Guidance, trusting you'll have what you need at the right place and time . . . when living in and from your "I"ntersection.

By letting go of these wants and following your Inner Guidance, you'll have each of them anyway as a natural result of living a life inside-out. You'll have true freedom, unconditional love, deep peace, personal control, internal and external approval, and security.

Your "Attention" . . . Is on Following Your Inner Guidance!

YOU'RE I-LIGNING YOUR ENERGY ON PURPOSE . . . IN THE MOMENT!

I owned property in the Oregon wine country and had a one-acre vineyard of pinot noir grapes that had a maximum yield potential of twelve hundred bottles of wine per harvest.

However, to get the best wine, the vineyard was thinned by cutting off a percentage of the green grape clusters early in the season to allow the remaining grapes to ripen faster and produce higher-quality grape juice. The energy put into the maturation of the vineyard was, therefore, concentrated on a smaller number of grapes. The result was 860 bottles of amazing wine each year to be shared with our friends and family. Without this thinning, the wine would have been lifeless and weak.

Without a thinning out and concentrated focus of the activities in your life, your life has been scattered and weak, with no real purpose. The quality of your life has been much less than it could be. Once you uncovered your "I"ntentions (Inner Purpose, Dynamic Possibility, "I" FEEL, "I" AM), you have a concentrated focus in your life. When you have choices to make, you have clearly defined intentions to guide you. Instead of randomly paying attention to everything, your attention is focused; you decide what to pay attention to and what to ignore. You thin out your life so you're focused only on those things that are contributing to the fruition of your intentions.

When you keep your "I"ntentions front and center by reviewing them first thing every morning and then creating your "Plan for the Day" (based on both the "I"ntentions and your Inner Guidance), you'll be allowing your Greatest Life to unfold in every moment.

Your "Attention" . . . Is on Living Intentionally!

YOU'RE OPEN TO OPPORTUNITIES SHOWING UP . . . IN THE MOMENT!

When you plant your seeds of "I"ntention in the field of the present moment, anything is possible. They're growing in an environment of unlimited possibility, and now the Universe is conspiring to help you bring them to life. Many opportunities will come your way!

By waking up grateful, you're setting yourself up to be grateful throughout the day for all the opportunities that are coming into your life . . . knowing they're showing up for your highest good. You stop being in resistance of these opportunities, especially those you have perceived as "bad." Instead, you welcome them to help you continue to evolve your Dynamic Possibility; to help you dissolve your shell; as a teacher, to help you learn something; or to strengthen your ability to ignore (or say no to) those things that don't support your journey to your Greatest Life.

By reviewing your "I"ntentions daily, you increase your awareness of the opportunities that show up in support of them. When I went to work for a bridge design firm during one of my college summers, I started noticing something I never paid much attention to before . . . bridges. They had been there all along but were invisible to me. During that summer, I noticed bridges everywhere, and each one required my observation and intense scrutiny. I saw each one as a potential opportunity for my company to repair or replace. When you begin to review your "I"ntentions daily, of all the billions of things happening around you, the ones that will conspire to help you accomplish your "I"ntentions will begin to appear in your awareness.

By keeping yourself present without expectations, you will see and recognize the opportunities when they present themselves to you. This is important, since the opportunities may appear in a form and at a time unexpected. They come from within, from your Inner Guidance, as "aha" moments, "knowings," or "nudges." They also come from life outside of you such as chance encounters with other people; a message you hear that gives you something you've been looking for; an infusion of a resource that allows a project to move forward; or a phone call from a friend or business associate with support you needed at that specific time. Before, when you were so lost in the past and future, opportunities were pounding at your door, but you didn't hear them . . . you were lost in time. Now you can.

Empowering the "I"ntersection" will allow you to see, hear, and act on these opportunities!

Your "Attention" . . . Is on Opportunities Being Drawn to You!

YOU'RE TAKING RIGHT ACTIONS . . . IN THE MOMENT!

Farmers need to constantly adjust their actions based on ever-changing, unpredictable conditions, especially due to weather. Sometimes the decision is a straightforward, common response. Many times, however, it's an intuitive decision among great uncertainty; they just know the right action to take.

"Right actions," in the context of I-Lignment, are defined as those actions (emotions, thoughts, words, and deeds) that fulfill your "I"ntentions, leading to your Greatest Life . . . in the service of others.

In each moment . . . by being clear on your "I"ntentions, by being present, being open to the opportunities as they come to you untainted by the past or future, and by listening to your Inner Guidance . . . you're setting yourself up to take right actions. You can "hear" what to do with the new opportunity, trust in that guidance, and then take the appropriate action without fear or reservation. You set yourself up to feel the "Right" emotions, think the "Right" thoughts, speak the "Right" words, and do the "Right" deeds.

You might be asking yourself why emotions and thoughts are included in the list of "right actions." Even though they can't be seen as external actions by people around you, their energetic impact can be felt by you and others. This can be proved through the coffee shop test mentioned earlier in the book. The action you take in choosing the emotions and thoughts you have internally will have a definite impact on the external world around you . . . and on how you show up in life.

There are five powerful checks to verify you are taking a right action:

- First, is the action in alignment with your purpose?
- Second, is the action taking you closer to or farther away from realizing your Dynamic Possibility?
- Third, is the action taking you closer to or farther away from the way you want to feel? (See your "I" FEEL list.)
- Fourth, is the action taking you closer to or farther away from the way you want to show up in the world? (See your "I" AM list.)
- Fifth, since right actions come from the inside-out, they have the same attributes as your authentic "I": deep peace, unconditional love, and true individual freedom. Is the action reinforcing these attributes in you and giving them to others? Is your action

coming from a sense of peace, love, and freedom, or is it coming from disempowering feelings associated with your shell, such as fear, guilt, and retaliation?

Taking only "right actions" empowers you to live a life of integrity. This is different from doing what the world thinks you should do or being honest. Doing what you know deep down is the right thing to do and is in alignment with your "I"ntentions is living with integrity . . . a life lived inside-out.

By Empowering the "I"ntersection daily, you're setting yourself up to take right actions in each moment, moving yourself toward your Greatest Life in service of others and bringing peace, love, and freedom into your life, the life of others, and into the world in general.

Your "Attention" . . . Is on Taking Right Actions based on Internal Guidance!

YOU'RE CREATING A POWERFUL VESSEL FOR YOUR JOURNEY . . . IN THE MOMENT!

There's a big difference between floating across the seemingly infinite, treacherous Pacific Ocean on a log raft going where the prevailing winds take you and hoping you make it to somewhere nice before falling apart and traveling on a sleek, hundred-foot yacht that will take you safely and comfortably to your destination of choice.

The yacht is specifically designed, constructed, and outfitted to make the journey across the Pacific. Its hull structure is built to slice through the water and withstand the constant pounding of the waves; its engine is powerful, so the yacht can consistently and without fail be propelled forward at a high rate of speed; its crew knows the purpose of the trip and are prepared with a navigation map and trip plan; its navigation system is robust to reliably handle all types of changing conditions and make the appropriate directional adjustments; and its interior is created for comfortable living.

You're building a similarly powerful, well-designed, and well-constructed vessel during your daily Empowering the "I"ntersection routine that will allow you to journey to and then live your Greatest Life.

During your daily routine . . .

- You discover the purpose of the trip during meditation . . . **your Inner Purpose.**
- You create your navigation map and trip plan during extended planning sessions . . . **your Dynamic Possibility and I-Ligned Life Plan.**
- You're guided on your journey by a navigation system . . . **your Inner Guidance.**
- You create an interior for comfortable living . . . **your Constant Release of Inhibiting Emotions and Beliefs.**
- You build a strong and powerful hull structure and engine for the journey . . . **your Peak Energy and Wellness Routine.**

We've discussed all of these except . . .

CREATING YOUR PEAK ENERGY AND WELLNESS ROUTINE

Having a strong and healthy body full of energy for your journey is critical. If you're to achieve your Greatest Life, this needs to be one of your high priorities. It's hard to reach your destination on a poorly constructed log raft.

Incorporating energy-producing and well-being activities within the daily Empowering the "I"ntersection routine is powerful. By doing this, you'll begin to perceive your physical well-being differently. Most people take care of their bodies from an outside-in perspective; they maintain their bodies to get approval, acceptance, and love from others. How they feel about themselves physically, no matter how great shape they get into, depends on the opinion of others.

You'll look at your physical well-being differently when put in the context of your "I"ntentions. The purpose of your physical well-being routine will not be to impress others but rather to create a strong vessel with high energy for your journey through life . . . to achieve your "I"ntentions . . . and your Greatest Life . . . having the ability to have many great experiences and adventures along the way . . . all the while serving others!

Your "Attention" . . . Is on Creating a Strong Vessel for Your Journey!

YOU'RE ENJOYING YOUR I-LIGNED LIFE . . . IN THE MOMENT!

True joy isn't found out in the world somewhere.

It's different from happiness. Happiness is fleeting; you experience it for a while, but it eventually goes away when something negative happens in your life, hopefully to return once again. Happiness is a feeling greatly influenced by your external life circumstances and the people in it, especially when you're living outside-in.

True joy is an intrinsic, internal state of being created by how you are "being" in each moment. If you're able to always be present and in presence, connected internally at a deep level to true individual freedom, unconditional love, deep peace, and living life inside-out following your Inner Guidance, then you will know an amazing inner joy that transcends anything outside of you. It's constant and independent of your life circumstances and the world around you. You'll always be in a state of joy, no matter what!

Empowering the "I"ntersection daily creates the conditions for this state of joy to emerge in your life.

From this inner joy, you see everything through the clear lens of your individual freedom, unconditional love, and internal peace. The world around you lights up as the fog of your inauthentic life dissipates! You see a real world that is alive, wondrous, full of opportunity, and abundant. You see there is so much to be joyful about in the world around you and use your attention to focus on those things. Your life expands into one of many amazing experiences and adventures . . . filled with love, connection, and passion!

Your "Attention" . . . Is on Enjoying Life in Each Moment!

As you continue the daily routine of Empowering the "I"ntersection, you'll experience your interaction with other people differently as well.

Living from your authentic "I" allows . . .

AUTHENTIC CONNECTION WITH OTHERS

Up to this point, the focus has been on you. But what about everyone else?

Other people have experienced the same process of developing their life described in "Why? Why Is My Life Like This?" . . . a life developed from the outside-in. They're living in and from their inauthentic shell with all its dysfunctional attributes and challenges. When these people then try to have a relationship with another person, both of their inauthentic shells, in effect, bump into and grind against each other. Because of the convoluted makeup of each shell and our propensity to judge others, the potential for friction, misunderstanding, and conflict is high. Having a sustained, authentic relationship under these circumstances is difficult.

When you understand and fully embrace this perspective, having compassion for others is much easier. They're struggling with many of the same challenges as you were . . . as they blindly continue to live an inauthentic life separated from their true self. Having this understanding and compassion is the first step toward an authentic relationship with anyone. Who they are authentically is not what you see on the surface; just like you, their authentic self lies beyond their shell at the "I"ntersection of their life . . . at "I."

WHAT ARE PEOPLE LOOKING FOR IN A RELATIONSHIP?

Having come to this point of your own transformation, you now know what was *missing* in your life when living in and from your shell and attempting to interact with others:

authenticity, presence, deep connection, wholeness, unconditional love, peacefulness, joy, freedom to be you, positive
energy, understanding, compassion, acceptance, and kindness.

Other people are no different. This is what is missing in
their lives as well. They're searching for these things in the
outer world, looking for others to provide them. Most of the
time, their search is not all that satisfying. The very people
they're looking to provide these things are looking for the
very same things missing in their lives as well. It's a vicious
circle of searching.

Because of this understanding and through the experience
of your own personal transformation, you can go beyond
their inauthentic shell and their reactions to life to begin to
form an authentic relationship with them.

You can also be, more importantly, a guiding light for
them, showing them how to achieve these things by living
life differently. You'll thus be a spark for their own transformation. As you know, they'll never deeply experience these
things until they rediscover and start living from their own
authentic "I." Then they don't have to look to others for the
things missing in their life . . . they'll already have them . . .
they'll already BE them.

TRUE CONNECTION . . . AT THE CORE

There's old advice used when trying to help someone interact with others more authentically; you're told to deal with
others "eye to eye." But perhaps that advice falls way short
of a much more powerful truth.

Don't interact with others "eye to eye"; interact with
them . . .

"I" to "I"

This is how you can see beyond their shell (including their dysfunctional reactions to life) and see the truth of who they really are at their core . . . their authentic "I." This is when real understanding and compassion are possible. You understand their plight and are willing to see beyond it. You're willing to connect with them "I" to "I" instead, even if they're not willing or capable of doing so themselves . . . yet.

FORGIVENESS . . . TO DISSOLVE THE WALL

The most important and powerful tool for transforming relationships and getting to an "I" to "I" connection with others is true forgiveness. It was discussed in the section "Dissolving the Shell" and is shown in Appendix C, "I-Lignment Meditation and Release Techniques." Rather than repeating it here, please go to the appendix and read, "I-Forgive I-Lignment Release Technique."

True forgiveness plays a critical role in transforming relationships with others in several ways:

- First, it allows you to release, during your journey inward to "I," the parts of your shell that are the accumulation of disempowering beliefs, emotions, and judgments about other people. They create an internal wall that separates you from others. Through true forgiveness, this wall within you is dismantled one brick at a time.

- Second, true forgiveness can be used on the fly to forgive others in any moment of conflict to prevent a buildup of beliefs/emotions/judgments to start forming a wall of separation once again. This is important, since most of the people you'll interact with in life will continue to live in and from their shell. They'll be triggered by and reactive to life . . . including to you. Your ongoing presence, understanding, compassion, and forgiveness will allow you to continue to have a deep, loving, and authentic relationship with them.

- Third, if you decide to part ways with someone, true forgiveness allows you to release on hard feelings, thoughts, and beliefs about the other person, so they don't linger in you and continue to impact your life. You are metaphorically releasing them and allowing them to go in peace while freeing you to go on living your life in peace as well.

True forgiveness is used, in this way, to pierce the veil of your own shell of distortion and to see beyond another person's inauthentic shell . . . to be able to know who they are in truth and make the connection with them there.

Then you can have . . .

DEEP, AUTHENTIC RELATIONSHIPS

You now have the power to have real and deep connections with the people in your life. You naturally bring into each of your relationships those things most needed and wanted by others.

Authenticity

There are three parts of authenticity in any relationship. The first two parts are your responsibility. The third part is up to the other person.

The first part you have already achieved at this point of I-Lignment—living in and from your authentic "I." You're living an authentic life on purpose and with "I"ntention . . . it's natural and real. People intuitively know you're authentic at a deep level.

The second part you have also achieved at this point of I-Lignment. You're able to see beyond the other person's inauthentic shell and connect with the authentic part of them . . . with or without their help. People can feel this intuitively as well, because you're different from most. You're not judging them based solely on their current behaviors, appearance, and life circumstances; they sense you're connecting with them, beyond all that stuff, at a much deeper level.

The third part is up to the other person. This is their own journey inward to "I" and the development of their ability to show up in relationships authentically as well as their ability to see beyond other people's inauthentic shell.

For you to have an authentic relationship with another person, the third part would be great but is not necessary. An authentic relationship happens when you connect with them "I" to "I" . . . connecting the authentic part of your life with theirs. At the same time, you understand and accept who they are in this moment living in and from their shell. This puts you in full control of creating an authentic relationship with anyone in your life . . . with or without their participation.

By approaching relationships this way, you directly or indirectly help others with the third part of authenticity. The other person sees how you're showing up authentically in life in general and in the relationship specifically and then starts reflecting on how they're showing up in life in comparison. Many times, this is the start of their own personal transformational journey.

People will be drawn to your authenticity!

Presence

Most people in our lives are constantly lost in time . . . thinking about the past or future. When you experience someone who is fully present, living in the present moment, and in total presence of you, that person stands out in the crowd. You feel a big need in your life being satisfied . . . you truly are being seen and heard.

Every day, through Empowering the "I"ntersection, you've been working at getting "outside of yourself" (out of your shell, where you were stuck, disconnected, and isolated from others) and focusing instead on staying present and in presence, both internally and externally. This daily repetition has strengthened that personal muscle. Now you have the ability to be present and in presence in every relationship in your life. You're interacting with others in the only time that is real and in the only place you can experience an authentic life together . . . right now!

By being in presence, you're giving them something they mostly lost early in their childhood and have had limited experience with since; it's a blessing to give that experience to them fully once again. You are being in presence with them and allowing them to be who they are in that moment, without judgment . . . allowing that moment in the relationship to be whatever it needs to be.

People will be drawn to your presence!

Deep Connection

People experience mostly shallow relationships with others in their life. They are dancing a dance with others on the surface of life; it feels inauthentic, and it is. It is why skin color is so important to so many people; the relationships they have are only skin deep. Each relationship is determined by the outer surface of the other person (physical characteristics, behaviors, life circumstances). Their relationship is with the other person's inauthentic shell. They don't know who the person really is.

You now have the insight and ability to go much deeper . . . to a relationship based on "I" to "I." It's a connection at the deepest level . . . at the very core of both of your lives. When you're connecting at this level, differences in skin color and other physical characteristics don't matter anymore. They seem superfluous. Also, current difficult behaviors and life circumstances are viewed not as things that define a person but rather as temporary, inauthentic conditions that can be changed to something much more authentic and loving.

You understand their current, challenging life in their shell and, at the same time, are connected to their true self. They might not yet understand these two parts of themselves, but they will intuitively know you understand and connect with them better than anyone else.

There's an Eastern greeting that captures the essence of this deep "I" to "I" connection between people . . . "Namaste." It means, "The divine in me bows to the divine in you."

People will be drawn to the depth of connection they feel when with you!

Wholeness

As described earlier, when people are separated from their true self through the formation of their inauthentic shell, they intuitively feel split and empty. They're living a life of duality; most of their life is lived in and from one part of their life, their shell, while the other part of their life remains mostly dormant, waiting to be rediscovered. As a result, they don't feel whole but don't know why. They then look to others to fill the void to complete them.

If two "not whole" people enter a relationship in order for the other person to complete them, it's a recipe for future difficulties. Expectations are formed, mostly unsaid, at the beginning of the relationship for what each person needs from the other to feel complete. When either one of them fails to get what they expected to fill the emptiness inside, there's disillusionment, and the relationship starts to suffer.

Since you've gone through the transformation of dissolving your shell and are now living solely from your authentic self, you feel whole. You don't need anything from anyone to complete you. Therefore, rather than showing up in a relationship appearing needy with many expectations, you show up as a giver with few expectations and a lot to share. In fact, with your newly discovered purpose and Dynamic Possibility focused on serving others, your whole life is now aligned to bring value into others' lives.

People will be drawn to you by how you show up solid and whole . . . as a giver rather than a taker!

Unconditional Love

At the heart of all relationships needs to be unconditional

love. Above all else, it's what everyone wants a lot more of and have been searching for most of their lives.

You were experiencing the same fruitless search for unconditional love from others until you went through your personal transformation and discovered the unlimited supply within you. When you're living in and from "I," you aren't just tapped into this supply; you're actually in a state of unconditional love.

All your relationships benefit. They'll be able to fill their empty love buckets when in a relationship with you if they're receptive. You'll easily be able to do this because you feel no limit to the amount of love you have to give. People in your life will easily experience the feeling of "being in love" when in your presence.

Your unconditional love is transformative as well. Love has the power to dissolve all the lower-level energies such as anger, hate, jealousy, and fear. Because most of the people you're in relationships with are still living in and from their shell, they'll continue to experience negative emotions, thoughts, and beliefs—and therefore be triggered often. With your unconditional love present, these disruptions to your loving relationship have a much better chance of being resolved and dissolved.

People will be drawn to you by the unconditional love they feel when in your presence!

Peacefulness

The lack of peace in a person's life is mostly caused by the disempowering, limiting, dysfunctional, and conflicting emotions, thoughts, beliefs, and stories retained in their shell from the past and used to imagine a fearful future. The deep and consistent peace that people desire can be experienced only at their "I"ntersection once they have learned to be present and in presence and have dissolved their shell.

You have done this. You're living from "I," which has deep peace as one of its constant states of being . . . independent of your life circumstances. You now bring a sense of peace into each relationship and all situations. You also have developed the ability to look beyond the chaos and noise on the surface of other people's lives and connect with them at the peaceful place that exists at their core.

People will be drawn to your deep sense of peace . . . a peace they long for in their own life!

Freedom to Be Them

True individual freedom is an inherent state . . . and a God-given right . . . at our very core.

But as a person's shell is constructed through the input of other people outside-in, that right is weakened bit by bit. Once the shell is fully formed, the control over a person's life has shifted to the shell's content and how that content automatically controls their thinking and behavior. Their life becomes mostly unconscious, reactive, and habitual. As they have been trained to do by then, they look outside themselves for guidance on what to do in pretty much every aspect of their life. In effect, they are controlled by the input of others from the past and present; their envisioned future is dictated by this input. Their individual freedom is all but obscured.

But the internal burning flame of "I"ndividual freedom never goes away. When they see someone who is living life independent and free, they long for the same . . . if not overtly, then secretly. They want their freedom back!

Through I-Lignment, you've rediscovered your true individual freedom! You found it once again at the only place it exists . . . the "I"ntersection of your life . . . at "I." Now you have infinite degrees of freedom with access to unlimited possibilities. By living a life of "I"ndividual freedom driven by your purpose and Dynamic Possibility, you become an inspiration to others.

You, through your own experience, now recognize that others have the right to their own "I"ndividual freedom as well. If you want true freedom for yourself, you need to allow true freedom for others . . . including the right to live a suboptimal life. This especially applies to the people closest to you . . . your life partner, your kids, your parents, your siblings, and your friends. Through this recognition, you become a great partner, parent, and friend; you encourage and support this freedom for them even if it disrupts your own life. You recognize that true individual freedom is an inherent right for all people!

People will be drawn to you as you freely live the life of your choice . . . and allow them to do the same!

Positive Energy

Most people believe all that we are is contained in our physical body, but it's not. Our life energy expands well beyond our physical body. If we're radiating negative, chaotic energy, we have a negative impact on life around us and add to the chaos of the world. If we're radiating positive, calm energy, we have a positive impact on life outside of us and bring more peace into the world.

Most people live from their shells; therefore, they're experiencing the chaotic, negative, limiting energy in their inner world and, as a result, are emitting the same to their outer world. This is why people so desperately want more positive energy in their lives.

You now are living in and from "I" and are radiating out into the world the energy from your core states of being . . . true freedom, unconditional love, deep peace, contentment, and joy. You're also projecting the energy coming from your clarity of purpose and Dynamic Possibility . . . the energy of calmness, sense of purpose, confidence, excitement, and passion. This combined energy is so different from the energy of most people; it's highly attractive to those in want of positive energy. They'll receive it by being in your presence. You can also be the impetus of them wanting to find the same within themselves.

People will be drawn, like a magnet, to your positive energy!

Understanding

People don't feel understood. Misunderstanding in a relationship is the source of so much conflict.

But now you understand why. The makeup of their life was from the uncoordinated input from thousands of sources. The result is a life that can be dysfunctional, conflicted, and confusing. It's difficult enough for people to understand themselves when living a life buried in their shell, let alone having someone else understand them.

With your new I-Ligned perspective, you can see the other person is clearly lost in their shell and is being reactive. Their behavior, appearance, and circumstances aren't who they are in truth. With this insight, you can remain calm and be inquisitive to understand what's really going on under the surface. All the while, you know their true self lies under it all at the "I"ntersection of their life.

People will be drawn to you because they feel heard and understood!

Compassion

People have a lack of compassion for someone when they believe a person's behaviors, appearance, and circumstances, while living in and from their shell, are who they are. They judge and form an opinion about others based on these three things. But you know now this is really their inauthentic self that is lost in and impacted by the dysfunctional, conflicted, confusing, and reactive nature of their shell.

You know because you've been there. You can feel their pain and confusion. You also know they're separated from their true self because you've had the experience of escaping your shell and are now living in and from your authentic "I." With this understanding, true compassion comes easy. You know that their struggles are like those experienced by everyone who still lives an inauthentic life from their shell. It's part of our human condition . . . until we individually decide to transform our life and shift the source of our life.

People will be drawn to you for your understanding and true compassion!

Acceptance

So many people judge how others are showing up in life, especially if the judgmental people are doing well. They believe the other person needs to be doing better.

You now recognize the importance of accepting everyone exactly where they are at any moment in their life. You've developed this insight through several of your own life experiences. First, every day during your daily routine (Empowering the "I"ntersection), you practice being present and in presence, both internally and externally. When you're present and in presence with the world around you, you see things as they are in the moment. Second, you've gone through your own personal transformation to realize your Greatest Life. You know it's an individual journey and at each moment in that journey you show up incrementally transformed. Where the other person is in their journey in life is perfect . . . for them. Acceptance of where they are in life is your only real choice and is the only choice that will lead to an authentic relationship with them.

People will be drawn to you because you accept them for who they are in that moment!

Kindness

Kindness is a natural outcome of being all the above things in a relationship. The other person will know you are a kind person and will feel the abundance of your kindness flowing into their life.

There is one thing that hasn't been mentioned that is important. When you're being all these things, you are full of joy. When you are joyful, laughter and smiles happen easily and often. Although laughter and smiles aren't required to be kind, they project your inner kindness and joy to the other people in your life and into the world in general. Don't underestimate the power of laughter and a kind smile to bring happiness into other people's lives. Smiles and laughs are an easy way to give your kindness away to everyone you meet.

People will be drawn to your kindness . . . to your joyful nature . . . to your smiles . . . and to your laughter!

Being of Service

People are surrounded by others that are self-absorbed. This is one of the traits when buried in and being impacted by the disempowering beliefs and emotions of their shell. Most of their energy is put into resolving the inner emptiness, lack of love, loneliness, conflict, discomfort, and fear they feel inside. As a result, many people have a tendency not to be there for others in their time of need.

You're different! Now that you've gone through I-Lignment and are living your life I-Ligned around your purpose and Dynamic Possibility, your life is all about being of service to others. The people in your life will see and feel the difference.

People will be drawn to you because they know their life is better when you're in it!

THE ULTIMATE RELATIONSHIP

In most of your relationships now, you'll be living an I-Ligned, authentic life, interacting with someone who isn't. As mentioned earlier, you can still have an authentic relationship with that person, but it's one-sided. You're bringing authenticity and its amazing attributes to the relationship; the other person is bringing mostly inauthenticity and many of the limiting and disempowering attributes to the relationship. These relationships can work (certainly better than when two inauthentic people are interacting), but they can also have their obvious challenges. The burden of the responsibility to have the partnership work well is on you and your ability to be understanding, compassionate, forgiving, peaceful, loving, and joyful.

The ultimate relationship is when both people have gone

through their own I-Lignment, independent of the other person, and are living their own authentic life driven by their purpose and Dynamic Possibility. When they then form a relationship that's synergistic, it's a powerful and loving union . . . its magical!

Imagine a relationship where both people come into it already possessing unlimited, unconditional love, a deep sense of peace and contentment, an underlying joy no matter what, a free and self-reliant spirit, a clear purpose for their life, and a clear understanding of the value they're bringing to the world in service of others.

Neither person is looking for the other person to complete them; they come into the relationship already whole. Neither person is desperately looking for unconditional love; they've each tapped into an unlimited source from within themselves and now radiate that love to others, including each other. Neither person is trying to go somewhere else to find peace in their lives; they've each already found it within themselves. Neither person is trying to escape to feel free; they've each discovered that freedom within themselves by escaping the prison of a time-based shell and by following their Inner Guidance. Neither person is uncertain in the relationship because each of them knows who they are, what their purpose in life is, and value they're giving to others.

Every person I've ever known who has had one of these relationships says the one thing that stands out is a feeling of contentment . . . no matter what. It's always present, no matter what they're doing with the other person. They feel whatever they're doing with the person and wherever there're doing it, it's perfect. They don't want to be anywhere else with anyone else.

You can certainly have this relationship with that special someone in your life, your life partner, but it becomes even more powerful when you have an ultimate relationship with many people in your life.

The Ultimate Goal . . . Oneness. This is the experience that we've all been searching for out there in the world. We've been looking for it in the wrong place. It's experienced when each person journeys to and then is living at their own "I"ntersection . . . their "I" . . . then joins, in relationship, with each other. An "I" to "I" relationship is formed that has *no* separation. You merge, in essence, into one "I." It's the ultimate relationship . . . a relationship formed in "oneness."

LET RELATIONSHIPS NATURALLY FLOW AROUND YOUR "I"NTENTIONS

I went through much of my life with a fear that was buried in my subconscious . . . the fear of being abandoned. Its origins were from my childhood, a feeling I inherited from my mom, who had experienced a lot of abandonment during her childhood and early adult years. As a result of this subconscious feeling, I wanted all my relationships never to go away. If they did, I would try my hardest to figure out if there was anything I did to cause the relationship to end and if there was anything I could do to bring it back.

Sometime during my own transformation I had several powerful aha moments that shifted my perspective. First, I realized I had a fear of abandonment and needed to release it . . . which I did. Second, I realized that relationships, except for one, were meant to flow into and out of my life. Some were meant to last a second, and others were meant to last a lifetime. Third, all these relationships always came into and out of my life for a purpose.

When my perspective shifted around these three things, my life started to flow much better. I stopped getting stuck trying to hang on to old relationships of the past and began allowing new relationships to flow in naturally. Fully accepting the ebb and flow of all my relationships opened my awareness of the rich opportunity each relationship offered.

Even though I had this new understanding, relationships would come into my life arbitrarily, and many didn't add to the quality of my life. In fact, some were downright disruptive, pulled me off course, and had a lot of negative energy that pulled me down. This led to several more important revelations that I realized were important parts of anyone's journey to their Greatest Life.

One Constant Relationship . . . Your Inner Source

The number one relationship in your life that needs to be a constant companion and guide, if you're to find and live your Greatest Life, is your Inner Source (Inner Power, Higher Power, God). It's the starting point for an authentic life lived inside-out.

From this relationship will flow everything you need and more! It's truly the source of unlimited wisdom, possibilities, unconditional love, and peace. Out of the relationship will flow your Inner Purpose, Dynamic Possibility, and I-Ligned Life Plan. It will also bring the right people and resources into your life at the right moment. By making this your primary relationship, all your other relationships will be more loving and peaceful . . . more authentic . . . more connected . . . more purposeful . . . more passionate.

It's also the one relationship that will always be there for you; it never goes away once you establish the connection. You'll never feel alone!

Make Your "I"ntentions Visible ... to Attract the Right Relationships

When you were living an inauthentic life that had no clear purpose or direction, relationships would come into your life in a haphazard way; they may have been attracted by the energetic pull of your chaotic, disjointed, and conflicted shell. You included people in your life who were attracted to that inauthentic person you were pretending to be. For the relationship to continue to work long term, you had to continue being a pretender. Your relationships were inauthentic and kept you stuck in that life. When new people came into your life, you had no clear way to decide whether to include the person into your life or not. You missed many opportunities to build amazing relationships that would have contributed greatly to your life, and you added people to your life who did not.

Once you created your "I"ntentions (Inner Purpose, Dynamic Possibility, "I" FEEL, "I" AM), you energetically put them out into the Universe to be fulfilled. You're now attracting those things that will bring them to realization ... including relationships. You can enhance this attraction by making everyone in your life (personally and professionally) aware of your "I"ntentions, letting them know you're committed to this path and are willing to do whatever it takes to realize them.

When you do this, the right relationships will flow into your life, seemingly out of nowhere, in the right moment. You'll also be much more aware when they do and see the opportunity they present. The other person will also benefit from the clarity of your "I"ntentions; they'll understand why being in a relationship with you is right for them.

You can also decide if there are relationships that no longer work and hold you back from pursuing your new direction in life. If you had a retail business and you started up a new manufacturing business, you wouldn't bring all the employees from the retail store over to run the manufacturing plant. Some may be part of that new business but not all. The same applies to starting your new life. Not all the people in your past life will be part of your new life. Your "I"ntentions can now provide a clear guide in making this difficult choice and help justify the decision. By letting some relationships go, you're making a clearing for the new relationships to come into your life.

The new, powerful relationships being attracted to you, aligned with your "I"ntentions, will be a big part of realizing your Greatest Life!

One note of caution: I'm sure people have told you, "Stay away from negative people." It seems like sound advice, but take a different perspective with your newfound wisdom. First, see each negative person who comes into your life as either a messenger to reflect one of your emotions or beliefs being triggered that you need to see and release; or as a person struggling in their own life, being triggered and reacting to the contents of their shell, and someone you could help. If, however, you find they're struggling with internal turmoil, want no help, and are benefiting in some way from continuing to be a negative person, then avoiding them may be best; you can't help someone who doesn't want to help themselves, and you don't want to have them constantly dragging you down.

By living an authentic life, on purpose, with "I"ntention, and in deep, loving connection with others, you create . . .

A PASSIONATE LIFE

I'm sure you've heard the phrase, "Follow your passion." Most people want to live a passionate life but have difficulty finding it. This happens because passion isn't achieved the way most people think; it isn't something you can find out in the world somewhere and then live. It's achieved as a natural outcome from living your life authentically from the inside-out, in alignment with your True Purpose, and focused on a Dynamic Possibility in service of others. The saying needs to be changed to, "Follow your True Purpose and possibility . . . a passionate life will naturally follow."

When living passionately on purpose, you'll jump out of bed each morning excited to start each new day in service of others! You're finally living your Greatest Life!!

When living your Greatest Life, you are . . .

CHAPTER TEN:
THE TRANSFORMED YOU

L IVING A LIFE that is incredibly beautiful and powerful!
This is how you now show up in life . . .

You feel authentic and real!

You're now living an authentic life. You've escaped the prison of your inauthentic shell (small "i") and are living from your true "I" . . . knowing it's the only place to discover authenticity and to live authentically. Your life has an internally discovered purpose. You're flowing and living inside-out, on purpose, and are living a self-created Dynamic Possibility. It's amazing . . . and transformative.

You also feel real. You're no longer living in the past or future; you're living now from your core . . . which is the only time reality exists.

You feel whole!

Your newfound wholeness has naturally resulted from the work you've done dissipating your inauthentic self. Before, when living life buried in your shell, you were separated from your authentic self, which lies at your inner core . . . the "I"ntersection of your life. It's only when you escaped the shell and traveled inward to your authentic "I," getting rid of the duality, that you rediscovered your wholeness.

And now that you have, only the one true you remains!

Your newfound freedom is real . . . with unlimited possibilities!

Isn't it amazing to finally be truly free?

Freedom is one of our most cherished and important goals. You can't attain your Greatest Life without "I"ndividual freedom. Your freedom has been finally discovered now that you're creating your life inside-out from the "I"ntersection of your life . . . a point in space with infinite degrees of freedom. At this "I"ntersection, you're no longer constrained by your inauthentic self living in time but, rather, are free to choose to go in any direction you want . . . and to tap into the vast reservoir of unlimited possibilities.

You also realize that freedom isn't something given to you. Freedom is a God-given right and is inherent in a life lived from your authentic "I."

Now you have the freedom to do the things you were destined to do . . . without constraint. You can create whatever life you envision . . . a life of greatness!

Your life is full of unconditional love . . . independent of anyone else!

You've finally found internally the unconditional love you have been endlessly searching for all your life out there in the world, where it's almost nonexistent. You turned inward and found an endless supply.

When you're at the "I"ntersection of your life, you're part of this unlimited source of unconditional love. Love is unconditional at the "I" because there is no condition required. It just IS unconditional love and is always present. You don't have to do anything to get it. You sink into a sea of unconditional love; you're immersed in it, and you inherently become it.

From this point, you don't need it from anyone else; rather, you radiate unconditional love out to the world in all directions. You now naturally attract others who are looking for unconditional love, and you help them discover the love that already exists within themselves. When you then both share a relationship of your merged unconditional love, the relationship is absolutely magical!

You experience waves of love coming from deep inside you!

Now that you're tapped into your endless supply of internal unconditional love, it easily gets triggered as you live your life. You find yourself having more and more experiences of love rushing to the surface in moments that are inspirational or touching. It'll come rushing up when you're feeling gratitude toward someone or something. You'll find the love easily present when you have a touching experience with another person or other living things.

Giving love unconditionally to others is now easy. Why not? You are unconditional love . . . you have an endless supply, and it easily comes to the surface when you're interacting with others. You instantly feel more loving, and you feel more loved.

You have a deep sense of peace . . . no matter the circumstances outside of you!

You're living in and from a place at your core that has, as two of its inherent states, a deep sense of peace and overall contentment. This sense of peace, therefore, is now a natural part of who you are.

You're living life from the inside-out . . . a life created from this place of peace. You understand that the chaotic life circumstances that surround you in any given moment do not define who you are. They are people and events outside of you, and you have the choice to be engaged with any of them . . . or not.

Your primary focus is on the present moment . . . the now of your life. The dysfunction, chaos, and drama of your time-based shell, which has been constantly disrupting your peace up until now with feelings such as regret, fear, guilt, anger, and worry, has been greatly dissipated. You're at peace knowing you can handle anything that comes up in any moment . . . especially with the perspective and tools you have learned from I-Lignment.

You live life powerfully . . . in each present moment!

You've learned a critical concept that has changed your life. The past is gone and the future isn't here yet; therefore, any attempt to make them real right now is an illusion. The only thing that is ever real is the present moment . . . right now. This is where life is to be lived and is the only place you have the power to live authentically and fully.

Out of the present moment, you're now flowing your authentic life from within . . . full of purpose and passion. In each moment, you're creating the life you want and, through that life, are bringing light and contribution to the world around you.

You have learned that if you experience and live life now . . . inside-out . . . life can be lived powerfully.

You have a whole new way of "being"!

You have taken to heart the saying, "We're human beings, not human doings." Rather than having a huge list of things to do to achieve a predetermined life in the future, you have a greater focus on how you're showing up in the world now. How you're "being" . . . now . . . is of utmost importance.

You are BEING in and living from the "I," the place where you're the most authentic, connected, and powerful . . . and this is where your life is unfolding in truly amazing ways. How you want to show up in each moment has become clear through the "I"ntentions you created, especially "I" AM _____.

You may be experiencing some or all of the following ways of being . . .

"I" AM ... Now.

"I" AM ... Truth.

"I" AM ... Kindness.

"I" AM ... Creative.

"I" AM ... Abundance.

"I" AM ... Real Power.

"I" AM ... Passion for Life.

"I" AM ... Unconditional Love.

"I" AM ... Authentic Connection.

"I" AM ... a Spark for Others' Success.

"I" AM ... a Life Created from the Inside-Out.

You've discovered the feelings you want in your life are the feelings inherently felt at your core . . . your authentic "I"!

During the process of I-Lignment, you uncovered the feelings you want once you achieve your Greatest Life. You've discovered many of these feelings are the same feelings you have when you live in and from "I" . . . from your true, authentic self. These are the feelings you're having when you're living inside-out on purpose.

You may be feeling some or all of the following . . .

- "I" FEEL . . . Authentic.
- "I" FEEL . . . Whole.
- "I" FEEL . . . Peaceful.
- "I" FEEL . . . Loving.
- "I" FEEL . . . Loved.
- "I" FEEL . . . Connected.
- "I" FEEL . . . a Close Relationship with my Inner Source, Inner Power, Higher Power, God.
- "I" FEEL . . . I'm in the Flow of Life . . . from Within.
- "I" FEEL . . . Free.

- "I" FEEL . . . Kind.
- "I" FEEL . . . Excited.
- "I" FEEL . . . Content.
- "I" FEEL . . . Joyful.
- "I" FEEL . . . I Contribute to Many People's Success.
- "I" FEEL . . . Successful.
- "I" FEEL . . . Accomplished.
- "I" FEEL . . . Abundant . . . in All Aspects of My Life.
- "I" FEEL . . . Physically Strong, Healthy, and Flexible.

You feel content!

You're content because you know you're exactly where you need to be, doing exactly what you're destined to do!

You experience an inner joy … that is independent of anything outside of you!

In the past, you thought joy was something you looked for

out there . . . somewhere in the world. What you've realized is that joy is a natural outcome of living in and from your authentic "I." You're experiencing it by being immersed in the attributes of "I" . . . deep peace, unconditional love, true freedom, and contentment.

You now know joy is different from happiness. Happiness, so often, is dependent on others and how they're treating you. People are fickle; therefore, so is your happiness. Because of this, happiness "forever" is a fallacy . . . it doesn't exist. However, continuous joy is real. Your worldly happiness is increased dramatically by realizing this inner joy and not relying on anything outside of yourself to achieve it.

Joy is now an underlying emotion that permeates all your life!

You have a newfound passion for life!

You wake up every day with a passion you've never felt before. It's a natural result of living a life on purpose and bringing to the world your Dynamic Possibility in service of others. You're seeing and feeling the positive impact you're having on the world in general and in the lives of specific people.

Living this way is creating a passionate life that never ends!

You're less impacted by the flow of life outside of you!

In your past, you thought "getting into the flow of life" meant getting into the flow of life outside of you . . . a flow created by others out there. Now you realize this was part of the problem; this perspective allowed other people or situations to control and impact your life and take you down different paths in life that made you feel inauthentic and out of alignment.

Now you're flowing your life from the inside-out. Your Source of Life is within you at your core. Based on your purpose and Dynamic Possibility, you now flow intentionally out into the world, creating an authentic life that is in alignment with your true self.

You don't let other people or circumstances sway you from the type of life you want to create; you pick and choose what and who, in the outer world, you want to get involved with as well as what and who you want to ignore. You accept the world for what it is . . . and don't take what's happening personally. You realize much of the dysfunction of the world is the collective dysfunction of the people who inhabit it. The positive change in the world can't be found in the world itself but, rather, first in your transformation, and then in the transformation of other people individually.

Therefore, the choices you make in life are no longer reactionary but very intentional, based on a bigger, internally generated Dynamic Possibility. Your life feels grounded and solid . . . even while living in an outside world of constant change, drama, and fear.

Your Inner Guidance has become your trusted source of powerful advice, not the multitude of people around you. The external world now has much less impact on and control over your life . . . even though you're still fully engaged in the world.

Your mind is clear and able to make quicker, better decisions!

Since you've dissipated your shell, there is less dysfunctional, conflicted, disjointed, and confused stuff from the past cluttering your mind. You've released it. You have a clearer space in your brain to accept fresh input and make decisions.

In the process of dissipating the shell, you've also shifted the source of your life from the prison of the inauthentic shell to a liberating Inner Source of unlimited possibilities at the "I"ntersection of your life. You've realized the importance of using this Inner Source as a powerful guide for making decisions and taking right action.

You've also learned that the feelings you want when living your Dynamic Possibility provides a tool to guide you in decision-making. You can ask, Is the emotion I'm feeling, the thought I'm thinking, the words I'm about to speak, or the actions I'm about to take moving me closer to the feelings I desire or taking me farther away?

Making decisions has become infinitely easier!

You're less reactive to the world around you; rather, you respond based on right actions!

Your shell is dissipated, and so is much of the shell's content that triggered your reactive and habitual behavior in the past. You're no longer ambushed by your emotional upheavals.

Now that the internal triggers are substantially reduced, you have space to make better choices and respond instead. You respond with right actions derived from your Inner Guidance. Since these right actions are derived from your Inner Source, they come from a place of love . . . rather than fear.

This is the true meaning of personal responsibility. You are responsible . . . "response-able" . . . "able to respond" from love rather than react from fear. Until getting beyond the shell, with all its conscious and unconscious emotional triggers, being truly responsible was difficult. Since you've done the I-Lignment work, you're now "responsible" and can take right actions in response to your interactions with the world around you.

You now know you can handle whatever life throws your way!

With I-Lignment, you have learned a new perspective, tools, and a process to transform difficult situations as well as to transform your entire life. You're no longer stuck in the prison of your shell; you have broken free and are living an authentic life from the inside-out. You know based on your own personal transformation, no matter what life challenges you encounter, you now have the power and ability to resolve them.

You look at the major events in life differently!

We all have had our own personal experience of, or have known someone who has gone through, one or more of the following major events in their life . . . falling in and out of love, bullying in school, physical/emotional/verbal/sexual abuse, accidents, divorce, unemployment, illness, alcohol and drug abuse, retirement, and dying. They have a big impact on our lives.

You used to view them as tragic. But now you view them

differently. They can still be painful, but now you see them as an opportunity and catalyst to transform either your life or another person's life. They are, so often, an interplay of two or more individual shells (small "i") clashing. When you don't understand this, all you see is the drama and pain of the situation and project blame outward. Now that you do understand this and can clearly see the clashing of shells, you can turn your attention inward, understand your reaction to the situation, release the inhibiting emotions and beliefs, tap into your Inner Source of wisdom, and then take right action. By doing this, you're taking personal responsibility in the situation and will be able to respond rather than react.

You've also realized you don't have to wait until the major life events happen before you, as stated above, "turn your attention inward, understand your reaction to the situation, release the inhibiting emotions and beliefs, tap into your Inner Source of wisdom, and then take right action." Instead, you have made this release a way of life; it occurs daily as part of your own personal transformation . . . your journey to and living from "I." Living this way will greatly reduce the occurrence of major life events. The buildup of emotional and mental turmoil and pressure, which usually leads to these major events, is released daily.

Many of the "wants" in your life have vanished!

When living in your shell, you felt that something was

missing. There was a void in your life. Something needed to be fixed. You were incomplete and you needed to add something to make you better and whole. As a result, a multitude of wants were generated from these uncomfortable feelings and your desire to fix them.

When you moved beyond your shell, released its grip on you, and started living from your authentic "I" instead, most of the wants either went away or the need to have them was greatly reduced. You now feel whole, complete, full of love, peaceful, and joyful, without any all-consuming neediness of anything outside of yourself.

You're simplifying your life!

Through the process of transformation, you've cleared the inner debris of your life. Your inner life has been decluttered and simplified; all the internal inhibiting emotions and beliefs have been released or greatly reduced.

When you decluttered and simplified your inner life, you have naturally wanted to declutter and simplify your outer world as well. The clutter around you became apparent and overwhelming. Your new mantra has become, "Simplify, Simplify, Simplify" versus "Buy, Buy, Buy."

You're now enjoying a simpler life . . . with much greater inner peace, free time, organization, flexibility, and mobility.

You have more natural abundance in all parts of your life!

When you were lost in your shell, feelings and thoughts of scarcity were always present. It seemed, no matter how hard you tried, you never got to the point where you had abundance in your life. You didn't have enough money, even if you were making a lot. Your relationships seemed to fall short of your expectations. You didn't have enough time to get everything done to get to a better life. Your life was far from peaceful. You didn't have enough love in your life. You felt empty inside; something was missing.

What you now know is that the lack of abundance reflected what was happening internally and was a natural outcome of living in and from the shell as your source of life. Now that you have escaped the limiting impact of the shell and are living a whole life from your true "I," you're experiencing real and ever-present abundance.

Abundance is happening because:

- You now need less because the cause of your wantings and desires to accumulate are gone or greatly reduced. Abundance has a lower bar to clear and is easier to achieve. You naturally perceive you have more without adding anything. Even getting rid of stuff gives you a feeling that you have more.
- You're no longer limited and constrained by your past. The energy you're projecting out into the world

is one of infinite possibility; therefore, opportunities are drawn to you. You're open to and allowing abundance to enter your life.

- You're living in the present moment, the only place you can discover the abundance that lies all around you.
- You've created a magnetic attraction for abundance to flow into your life through the creation of your "I"ntentions.

Abundance has become your way of life . . . it's infused in everything you think, say, do, and experience. You're living in a world of abundance that you're tapped into. You're now receiving things you need when you need them. You're getting calls from or meeting people at the right time for the right reason. You get opportunities handed to you. These seeming "miracles" are more commonplace and expected in your life.

Your life feels more effortless and enjoyable!

You've escaped your inauthentic, dysfunctional, disjointed, conflicted, demanding, needy, and confusing shell that has created an incredible amount of stress, anxiety, uncertainty, and fear in your life. The dramas and regrets of the past and the projection of the past into a fearful future are no longer dominant in your life. The effort and time spent dealing with this internal conflict is gone. Not only have you escaped your anxiety-ridden, time-consuming, and energy consuming shell, you now have the I-Lignment perspective and tools to deal with anything else that comes up in life.

You're living an authentic and "I"ntentional life aligned around your purpose and Dynamic Possibility . . . lived in the present moment. You have a newfound freedom, living a life flowing from the inside-out . . . following a trusted Inner Guidance that makes right actions clear. Making decisions and taking empowering actions with your newfound energy and extra time is so much easier.

Your life is finally your own. Life flows unrestricted from within . . . with a deep sense of peace, unconditional love, and contentment. Knowing that you are living your Greatest Life makes life effortless and enjoyable!

Your relationships are deeper and more authentic!

It's difficult to have a deep and authentic relationship with others when your inauthentic shell is bumping up against their inauthentic shell. It's a relationship on the surface of life. Your thin facade is interacting with their thin facade.

Since you have done the work to get beyond your shell and started living from your authentic "I," at the "I"ntersection of your life, you've realized how true this had been for you. Now as you interact with others, they experience your authenticity.

They sense your deep peace. They feel your unconditional love. They experience your undivided presence. They see how joyful you are. They admire your passion and confidence as you pursue your purpose in life and bring your possibility to reality. Most are drawn even closer to you. You're like a beacon of light in a sea of inauthenticity.

This deep and authentic relationship happens even if they're still lost in their own shell. Because you have been through your own personal transformation, you can see the other person's plight living inauthentically from their shell. You, therefore, don't react to their behavior, you forgive them, you look beyond their shell to their true self at their core, and then you respond to them, coming from the peace, unconditional love, and joy you bring to the relationship.

As a result, your relationships are transforming, and the change is showing up in different ways. The interactions you're having with people you care about are deeper and more real. You're more understanding, compassionate, and patient with others. There's more love present in all your relationships. You're at peace with others in your life, including the difficult people. You don't attack others; you're a uniter, not a divider. Your relationships are a lot more joyous, filled with smiles and laughter. Your radiant energy of unconditional love, peace, and inner joy is attracting many amazing people into your life. Your "I"ntentions are attracting the right people who support your life's journey; people who don't support your journey fade out of your life. Your neediness for specific relationships to happen has gone away; instead, you're simply allowing the right relationships to be attracted into your life. You no longer seek approval from others, nor do you expect them to have your approval. You love all people more and are accepting of how other people show up in life.

Your experience of "falling in love" with someone is now powerful and unconditional!

The true meaning of "falling in love" is finally understood. Before you thought, as do most others, falling in love meant a love you felt to and from another person; it was dependent on someone else. Now you know when you are falling in love with another person, you each individually are falling into your own inner sea of unconditional love at your core.

Since you have gone through I-Lignment, you have fallen in love within yourself . . . within your true self. You dropped into this sea of unconditional love and became it. You now radiate it in all directions indiscriminately. This allows you to easily be in this state of unconditional love for and with many others. They can feel it and are drawn to your love.

You've become more accepting of others . . . as they are!

It's easy for you to have compassion and empathy for other people now that you've escaped your inauthentic shell and, with your newfound vision, can understand their plight. You're more accepting of them because you understand that their behavior and circumstances are a reflection of the dysfunctional, conflicted, and confusing content of their shell, which was mostly an outside-in creation given to them by others. They've come to believe it's who they are and don't even know there's an alternative. They don't understand the source of their difficult life circumstances is internal, and they are, therefore, pointing their blame outward.

Even though their behavior may be difficult to deal with, you understand how they have come to this point and why their behavior is so reactive. It doesn't mean you necessarily condone their behavior, but you can accept them as they are in that moment. You know, from your own experience, their amazing true self is buried just below the surface, waiting for them to discover . . . when they're ready.

You allow unlimited possibilities for others . . . beyond your own self-interests!

When you were living a life outside-in from your shell, you felt incomplete, not whole, limited, and not good enough. You saw others as a means of making your life better. They were part of the solution to your woes; therefore, you needed them to play a particular role in your life that would provide relief or fill in a certain part of your life where you felt incomplete. If they deviated from that role, you may have objected strongly and resisted their efforts to change. They weren't doing what you needed and expected them to do . . . for you.

Now that you have rediscovered your authentic self "I," you feel complete and whole at your core. You feel a deep peace and contentment. Unconditional love, the one thing you had desperately searched for from others all your life, is available in unlimited quantities from within. You're living your life inside-out and deriving your guidance and power from within, not relying on the outside world for that power and guidance. You're no longer trapped by time and, instead, are living life in the present moment. All of this allows you to be tapped into a source of unlimited possibilities.

From this powerful place, you've let go of your neediness of others and your expectations that they show up in your life in a particular way . . . if at all. Your efforts to restrict their lives to meet your needs is gone. You now see and want for them a life of unlimited possibilities . . . allowing them to live their Greatest Life.

You express many acts of kindness in your daily life!

When you become unconditional love, a natural attribute

of living in and from "I," and combine it with an under-standing of people's dilemma living in and from their shell, it's easy to be kind to others. Kindness becomes who you are always . . . not some exception. You wouldn't think of acting any other way.

Your life is spacious and light!

Living in the shell can be very dense, dark, and heavy. As you went through I-Lignment transformation, the shell became more spacious as you let go of inhibiting emotional charges and beliefs. The light began to shine through, and your world became increasingly brighter. At your "I"nter-section, your inner light now shines incredibly bright, and your life feels light and spacious.

Your well-being is a natural state . . . not something you need to work at!

"Dis-ease" in your body is a major contributor to disease in your body, as well as to a lack of well-being in your life in general. Your shell was filled with content that generated dis-ease.

As you've gone through the I-Lignment process, you've

released or dissolved much of the shell and its content, such as disempowering and conflicting beliefs, inhibiting emotions, and disempowering stories. As you took away this source of dis-ease, many of the debilitating symptoms that had been showing up in your life went away as well. Anxiety and stress are much less and are replaced by feelings of peace and calmness. Aches and pains simply go away. Tightness in the chest and muscles relax. You get fewer or no colds or flus. Difficulty in breathing goes away. A hurting heart is instead bursting with feelings of love. You lose weight without trying. Your habitual behaviors many times just cease.

In addition, you're behaving differently and in ways that enhance your well-being. You're taking an aware interest in what you eat and drink, what you put on your skin, and what is in your environment. You're exercising more and in ways that enhance your well-being, not just to build muscle or to make yourself look good. You're taking more time to relax and have adventures. You meditate regularly to be present and to make a deeper connection with your Inner Power to get guidance. You have a strong desire to get out and connect with nature.

You're now experiencing a natural, vibrant well-being . . . from your core out.

Your inner discomfort or pain that drove your compulsive behavior is gone!

When you were living with habitual and compulsive behaviors driven by an internal discomfort or pain, your life was not your own. You were continuously triggered by life and reacted automatically. You were literally on autopilot.

Through I-Lignment, you have released or dissolved the inhibiting emotional charges and disempowering beliefs that created your discomfort and pain and caused you to react. When they went away, so did your habits and compulsions. There was no reason for them to exist anymore.

Now you're choosing to respond instead driven from a different Source of Life . . . that is peaceful, joyful, and full of love.

You're enjoying peace and quiet!

When your life was full of emotional and mental baggage, you engaged in endless ways to sedate and control the pain and discomfort it created. When you finally released and dissolved all the emotional and mental baggage, the need to do anything in response went away.

You're now living from a place at your core that is at peace and full of love. Your outer life has become peaceful, quiet, and loving as well . . . a reflection of your new inner condition.

You now feel comfortable in quiet and peaceful settings, with nothing to do but just be. Quiet alone time before felt uncomfortable . . . especially for any long period of time.

Now you enjoy your alone time . . . relish it, in fact. You enjoy being by yourself in solitude . . . especially in nature.

Thoroughly enjoying solitude and alone time with no one to see and nothing to do is a clear sign you're living authentically at the "I"ntersection of your life.

Your energy has increased dramatically!

The dysfunctional nature of the shell demands an incredible amount of energy and attention to cope with it and make sense of its convoluted nature. Even making simple decisions is difficult because its makeup is so conflicted and confusing. Living in the shell sucks the energy right out of you. It's like a dark hole in space.

Your energy has now increased dramatically after I-Lignment for three primary reasons:

First, as you journeyed inward out of your shell and to your authentic "I," your level of consciousness increased along the way. Each new level of consciousness brought with it a higher energy level. Now that you're living at the "I"ntersection, you're living in the very high energy levels of unconditional love, deep peace, and joy. High energy is a natural attribute of living in and from your authentic "I."

Second, as you moved from your shell, the dense hole that was sucking away your energy is dissipated or gone. You no longer lose energy being angry, fearful, regretful, holding grudges, seeking approval, searching for love, attacking, trying to rectify the past, or trying to control the future.

Third, life is so much easier and requires much less energy as you align your life around your "I"ntentions. You allow the Universe to help you bring it to reality. You can then trust and relax, knowing it will happen at the right time.

You have a deep sense of power you've never felt before!

You've been taught from a young age that the power you needed to plug into to be successful in life was out there somewhere in the world. Someone else had it, and you needed to tap into it.

Now you know the real power exists deep inside you. It exists at the "I"ntersection of your life. It is and always has been there and is accessed only in the present moment . . . right now. Now that you've tapped into it, it's giving you all the power, wisdom, and resources you need.

You have a personal connection with your Inner Power!

You're now connected to your Inner Source . . . your Inner Power!

Once you've tapped into and experienced even a glimpse of this Inner Power, you want more. You want this power to flow through you unrestricted.

More of your attention has become focused on spiritual exploration and integration into your life. You're tapped into something much greater than you alone. You're tapped into infinite power, infinite possibilities, infinite resources, and timelessness.

You now connect with your Inner Power daily . . . as a "way of life."

You trust and follow your Inner Guidance!

You've shifted your guidance from outside-in to inside-out. Your Inner Voice is clear now and is giving you constant guidance; you're fully trusting and following it. From the guidance, you're taking "right action" even if it alters your current plans or goes against the opinions of others.

Doing the intuitively right thing is at the core of who you are now and how you show up in the world!

You don't need approval from others!

Through I-Lignment, you've let go of wanting approval. You know you don't need approval from anyone if you're following your Inner Voice and taking right action in each moment, allowing your "I"ntentions to unfold. You're creating your own life based on your purpose in life . . . in a way that brings tremendous value to many people and the world around you.

You feel empowered . . . you're no longer a victim of life!

You may have been a victim when you lived an outside-in life. You were taught, as you grew up, to live your life in the flow of others out there in the world. They had the power and control over your life, not you. Therefore, when things happened in your life, especially negative things, you viewed the cause as being outside yourself. You projected your blame and anger outward. Even more disempowering, you relied on them to change before your life could improve.

You've now completely rejected being a victim! You realize that a difficult life is mostly a reflection of your inner emotional and mental turmoil. Through I-Lignment, you have done the work to move beyond the chaos of your shell and are now living from your Inner Power. Your life is flowing from this power from the inside-out. You know you're totally empowered to create the type of life you want to create! And you're doing it! You're doing it powerfully!

You're committed to your purpose … something much greater than just yourself!

It was difficult to find your True Purpose when buried in your shell, because you were greatly influenced by others and were, consciously or subconsciously, looking to others to help you find it. Your possibilities were also limited and constrained because of the inherent constraints of the shell and the people around you holding you back.

When you escaped the prison of your shell and discovered your authentic "I," your world expanded dramatically. All things were possible. When you started creating a life from "I" and got your guidance from within, your True Purpose naturally came to light. You knew it when it appeared.

You discovered your purpose in life selfishly (you had to discover what it was for yourself, by yourself, with no external influence), and now you're executing your purpose and Dynamic Possibility out into the world unselfishly. Your True Purpose now aligns your life in this world to do your part in being of service to others.

Your creativity has been empowered!

When you lived a life outside-in, there really was no true creativity; it was copying. You looked to others out there for everything you did. Since most people you got your guidance from lived in a world of time where everything is constrained by their individual and shared remembered pasts and projected futures, the number of possibilities given to you were constrained and limited as well.

Now that you're living inside-out, you're free of the outside-in limitations/restrictions and are tapped into your true inner creativity and unlimited possibilities. True innovation and transformation are now unleashed and will continue to blossom in your life and through your contributions to the world!

Your life is created . . . inside-out!

You're now the creative director of your life. Life is flowing from the inside-out from your Inner Source, a source that is unlimited. You have true freedom to create any life you want.

You look at what might go right in life … as opposed to what might go wrong!

When you were living in and from your dysfunctional, conflicted, and confusing shell, along with everyone else, you experienced a lot of chaos and drama. Many times, life just didn't make any sense. It was very confusing and inconsistent. Many things went wrong. You were physically, verbally, or mentally attacked by others. From these experiences, you built up your walls of defense against attack and what might go wrong.

Now that source of dysfunction is gone or greatly reduced. You've been able to lower the walls of defense that you had erected. You're now living a life that seems real and is flowing from you. You're taking personal responsibility and are being proactive in making things happen based on your "I"ntentions. You're tapping into your Inner Guide daily and, based on what you "hear," are taking right action. Your trust in your Inner Guide is paying off; your life experience is great. So many more things are going right and are powerfully moving your life forward. You have an optimistic view on life in general.

You've adopted the perspective, "Life is powerfully working for me!"

Your life is more about contribution, adventure, experiences, and people … rather than the accumulation of stuff!

Since you've cleared the debris from your shell and started living from a place of authenticity, unconditional love, and unlimited possibility, your life has become an amazing adventure as you live your life's purpose.

Accumulation of possessions to fill an emptiness you felt inside isn't important anymore. Stuff just weighs you down and makes your life feel heavy and dense. You want lightness and flow now. You're focused on keeping life simple; you've realized that simplicity is one of the keys to inner joy and happiness.

Life is now about adventure, experiences, people, and contribution … all flowing into your life as you allow your purpose and Dynamic Possibility to unfold in the world.

Life has become your playground!

The world you saw before was a reflection of the dysfunction of your inner world, which had been created for you up to that point. You were impacted and controlled by the world around you. It was not so fun.

Now you're flowing life from within . . . from your place of all possibility. Now it's become exciting and fun. The world is your stage where you, as the director of life, can create the theatrical play of your choosing. Your inner creativity has been unleashed. You look at life as a constant exploration without knowing for sure what's going to happen next. It's a creative journey of your choosing without a final destination; you just flow from one amazing scene of your play to the next. You play more, laugh more, and are more joyful.

You've put yourself into a position to have many wonderful experiences . . . with people . . . with destinations . . . with exploring the world . . . with contributing to others . . . in those special moments in life that you come across and just go with because you have the openness and flexibility to do so.

Life has become your playground!

You feel "connected" with life!

Being "connected with life" takes on a whole new meaning and significance now that you have journeyed to and are living from your authentic "I."

Before, you were lost in the inauthenticity of your shell. You were separated from everything by virtue of the shell.

It hid your true self, it separated you from an authentic connection with others, it kept you trapped in time and out of the present moment, it blocked your Inner Power, and it blocked you from living your Greatest Life.

Now your life is authentically connected . . . and it all merges at the "I"ntersection of your life . . . right now in the present moment. You're connected to your innermost, true self "I." You're connected to your Inner Power, Inner Source, Higher Power, God. You're connected to your Inner Purpose. You're connected to the flow of your creativity from your Inner Source out into the world. You're connected to a Dynamic Possibility that allows you to make your purpose come true in the world by being of service to others. You're connected to others, seeing beyond their shell to their authentic "I."

You finally feel connected to who you really are . . . and how you were meant to show up in this world!

You feel a oneness . . . with all life!

Oneness is a term used when talking about bringing people together in harmony and to improve relationships between groups and the world in general. As people live their lives today, it may work for a short while, but it never seems to last very long.

Now you really understand what oneness means and where it can be found. It isn't out there somewhere. It's found at the "I"ntersection of your life with another person and then with many others. It only happens as you journey inward into your own oneness at your authentic "I" and then as you join with others who have found their own oneness themselves. Separation caused by each of your respective shells is gone, and you come together at "I" . . . the place of deep peace and unconditional love.

From oneness, you see and experience the connectedness of all life. You find yourself increasingly drawn to and deeply resonating with other people and nature . . . naturally wanting to bring peace, unconditional love, understanding, and compassion into each encounter.

You have become part of the possibility of the world eventually experiencing oneness! A world radiating unconditional love, deep peace, and true freedom!

You naturally want to create a better world!

You understand, especially through your own transformation, that to change the world you must first change *your* world. It's an inner journey we must all first take. You have taken the I-Lignment journey and are living life from your own oneness.

From this place of oneness, you can clearly see the plight of others as they continue to struggle in their respective shells, all separated from each other. You now understand why they behave the way they do, individually and in groups, and how they got there. You feel compassion toward them. You have a strong urge to want to help make things better.

One way you are helping is by showing up differently in the world than most others. Because you're living life from your authentic self, you inherently radiate into relationships or situations, authenticity, peace, unconditional love, joy, understanding, and compassion. You show up in a way that allows solutions to issues to emerge from the right place. You bring light to show the way!

You also help by getting directly and actively engaged in situations that are in alignment with your Inner Purpose. It's different, though, than the way you used to contribute. Before you used to see a change that needed to be made, according to you, and went about trying to change things forcefully and, many times, backed by indignation, righteousness, anger, frustration, impatience, and sometimes downright hatred and violence. Now you put an "I"ntention into the Universe and wait for an opportunity to arise to be involved in a transformation, all the while staying in presence and being authentic, peaceful, unconditionally loving, joyful, understanding, and compassionate. These opportunities show up in the right moment to allow you to contribute naturally in big or small ways.

You have transformed into a life of being of service to others . . . and being a shining light to the world!

You're now powerfully living your Greatest Life in every moment!

CHAPTER ELEVEN:
"I" ... AUTHENTIC YOU FOREVER!

"I" AM the Rock in the midst of the raging sea,
that is a symbol of an empowered life that is free.

"I" stand firm against the forces of wear and tear,
showing the importance of Love and Peace for all to share.

My power is radiated from my inner core,
and is felt by those who are in want of more.

"I" bring contentment and joy to those standing in awe,
of my infinite wisdom and irrefutable law.

—RON MANSETH

You've become the "Rock" in the raging sea of life by living your life different from most. You aren't getting your inauthentic power from the raging sea around you, but rather you're creating an authentic life from a new, peaceful source, deep within you. That outer chaos is no longer reflected within you; you're calm. You've fallen into an inner sea of unlimited, unconditional love that you now radiate out into the world around you. You've connected with, are trusting, and are following your Inner Guidance. Out of that guidance has flowed your purpose in life and the Dynamic Possibility you're bringing to the world. You've discovered a freedom you never thought you had to live a life of your creation. Your life is one of incredible vitality and passion!

You're living this new authentic life in each new present moment! It has become your new way of life . . . a life that can go on forever without end because it's flowing from within . . . inside-out!

You're now able to naturally change three important perspectives that have been distorting and constricting your life . . .

YOU'LL NEVER "RETIRE"!

When I was in my latter twenties, I kept meeting people in their late eighties and early nineties who owned their own businesses. Most of them had acquired enough wealth to be retired, be independent, and do pretty much anything they wanted. But they were still going into work every day! I was perplexed. I asked them, "Why are you still working? Why don't you take off and travel the world? You're rich!" Each time the reply was, "I love what I do! Why wouldn't I go into work! It's my passion!"

At the same time, I watched people work all their lives, doing jobs they hated because they paid well and had good health and retirement benefits, so they could finally live "the good life" once they retired. What they really wanted by retiring was to escape their current life. After dedicating all those years to this suboptimal life, retirement finally came, only to have a health, financial, or relationship crisis completely disrupt their plans. Sadness and disillusionment followed.

From these experiences, I had three revelations. First, I realized waiting to finally live the "good life" in retirement was ridiculous and led to regret. I decided never to retire and live my life in each and every moment! Second, from these inspirational older people, I realized that my life was best lived doing something I'm passionate about and that I love to jump out of bed to do every morning! Third, I realized the difference between the people just doing a job to retire at sixty-two and the entrepreneurs still working at ninety was that the latter had a purpose for what they did every day of their lives and were creating something of value they were bringing into other people's lives.

The people just working a job with no purpose other than to retire seemed to grow old early while the people with a sense of purpose and a Dynamic Possibility in service to others were still living a passionate and dynamic life! They were still youthful at ninety!

Having gone through I-Lignment, you're positioned to be the person who is thriving for the rest of your life . . . never retiring . . . only living your Greatest Life . . . always!

YOU'LL NEVER "DIE"!

Everyone I've ever known has had some fear of dying. Everyone wants to escape the aging process and death. It's ingrained in our culture. An enormous number of products and services are created to arrest the aging process and death of our bodies. The incessant focus and fear are because many people believe we are our bodies, and when it dies, so do we.

But it's not true. We're not just our bodies; we're so much more. Infinitely more.

You understand this as you experience journeying to and then living from your authentic "I." You lose your fear of and focus on the future and death, knowing that your life doesn't end with your body. Instead, you focus on living to the max now! You experience living anew . . . being refreshed . . . being fully alive . . . in each and every moment.

Living this way has now empowered you to stay young . . . forever!

YOU'LL TREAT LIFE AS A JOURNEY . . . NOT A DESTINATION!

Through I-Lignment, you realize how the concept of waiting until you retire has kept you from living your Greatest Life. You now realize the "golden years" are possible right now . . . if you live life I-Ligned with your "I"ntentions . . . and treat life as a journey of one present moment followed by another present moment ad infinitum.

You've become a traveler and adventurer down the pathway of life into eternity . . . blazing your own trail. You've put yourself in position to have many wonderful experiences in each moment . . . with people . . . with destinations . . . with exploring the world . . . and through those special,

simple moments in life, you come across and just go with
. . . because you have made the "time" to do so.

You're living your Greatest Life at each step of your life's
journey!

**You're now empowered to make an incredible difference
in the world . . . for the rest of your life . . . and beyond!**

PART FOUR:
CREATING A NEW WORLD

CHAPTER TWELVE:
CHANGE YOUR WORLD . . . CHANGE THE WORLD

LET'S TRANSFORM OUR WORLD INTO A BEAUTIFUL PLACE!

You now understand the truth behind the statement mentioned at the start of the book, "The Transformational Journey to "I" Is Critical to You and the World . . . Because You're Always Creating."

You create . . . every day . . . every hour . . . every minute . . . every second. With every emotion you feel, every thought you think, every word you speak, and every action you take, you're shaping your life and the world around you. The outcome depends on the creative source. Right now, the most common source is each person's shell individually and from all our shells collectively. What's showing up in the world reflects these outside-in sources of life . . . inauthenticity, dysfunction, chaos, conflict, anger, conditional love, manipulation, wars, struggle, and fear. As we raise our kids, the source of their learning comes mostly from this pool of people as well. We create a whole new generation of humans who live outside-in, inauthentic, and disempowered lives. If we all keep creating from this source, we'll get more of the same.

> *"You must be the change you wish to see in the world."*
> —*MAHATMA GANDHI*

But we all have a choice! We can choose instead to rediscover our authentic "I" and live life inside-out . . . living beautiful, authentic, and free lives filled with unconditional love, peace, contentment, and joy. We can bring our purpose and possibility that each of us was meant to fulfill in this life . . . in service of others . . . leading to a passionate life. We can have deep, authentic relationships with each other . . . connecting "I" to "I" . . . bringing into all our relationships unconditional love and a deep sense of peace. We can choose love over fear . . . peace over war.

It's up to each of us individually—and then collectively. The journey to transform the world is first an internal journey you must take yourself. Only then can you, by the way you show up in the world, begin to make a transformational difference. As more of us make this choice, the world will increasingly reflect this shift.

INDIVIDUAL FREEDOM . . . OUR ONLY PATH!

To make this choice, you must have "true individual freedom." The only place you'll find this freedom is at the "I"ntersection of your life . . . at "I." From "I," you have the freedom, power, and unlimited possibilities to show up differently in life and to start transforming the world around you.

As a society, we must recognize the importance of true individual freedom and support it for all of us. Without it, there will be those in power who, acting from their dysfunctional shells, will want to dictate how all of us live our lives. If we allow it, our dysfunctional world will continue and get worse. It will restrict our freedoms and increase separation. We must individually journey to "I" to find this freedom for ourselves and then fully support all others to do the same.

True individual freedom is the heartbeat of an authentic and beautiful life! True individual freedom is the heartbeat of an authentic and beautiful world!

ONENESS

We now have a free path to the elusive oneness . . . the unity we so long for!

Up to now, we've all been looking for oneness in the wrong place . . . out in a world where it doesn't exist. The very nature of each person's shell creates separation. As long as our thick, impenetrable shells exist, true oneness is not possible.

"On the surface of life is where all separation is found . . . and oneness will never be found."

The only way for us to come together in oneness is for

each of us individually to first journey to our authentic "I," where oneness (wholeness) is discovered for ourselves. We can then experience shared oneness through "I" to "I" relationships . . . all flowing from the same Inner Source. Our shared oneness expands as more and more people join in "I" to "I" relationships . . . formed from unconditional love, deep peace, individual freedom, contentment, and joy as the basis for everything we do together.

But oneness isn't limited to people. When living in and from "I," we're able to feel the oneness with all life around us . . . the underlying connection with all living things. Feeling this expansive oneness opens us to an infinite, amazing world beyond our wildest imagination.

CHANGE THE WORLD!

Now you know we all have the power individually to change the world into the beautiful world we so desire. All each of us needs to do is make a committed decision to start down the journey of I-Lignment so we can live a life in and from our authentic "I" . . . to bring our Greatest Life to share with the world . . . and join forces with others doing the same.

We now have the opportunity to transform our world into a phenomenal place!

One of deep peace, unconditional love, true individual and shared freedom, infinite creativity, and unity!

One person at a time . . . starting with you!

PART FIVE:

YOUR TRANSFORMATION JOURNEY

CONGRATULATIONS! YOU'VE COME to the point where you have a powerful new perspective that will allow you to transform your life! You're ready to start your journey to live in and from your authentic "I" . . . living your Greatest Life from the inside-out!

You'll now be guided through the I-Lignment process. It will be synergistically integrated with the concepts introduced in the prior chapters.

The I-Lignment process is divided into eight steps:

- Step 1: Shift Your Perspective.
- Step 2: Empower Your Journey.

- Step 3: Ask: Where am "i"?
- Step 4: Create Motivation . . . the "Big Why."
- Step 5: Create an Interim Dynamic Possibility and Plan.
- Step 6: Journey to "I."
- Step 7: Create Your Greatest Life . . . from "I."
- Step 8: Create a New World.

Before you begin your transformation, consider this . . .

It's been said, "People overestimate what they can accomplish in one year, but way underestimate what they can accomplish in ten." Each year has 365 days. There are 1,440 minutes in each day; therefore, there are 525,600 minutes in each year. In ten years, there are a total of 5,256,000 minutes. If each minute represents a "present moment," there are 5,256,000 present moments. Let's take it one step further. Determine the age you think you'll live to, subtract your current age, and then multiply that number by 525,600. That's the number of present moments you have for the rest of your life. If you're forty-five years old and believe you'll live until you're eighty-five, this means you have 21,024,000 present moments left in your life. Imagine what you could do with all those present moments to make a massive difference in your life, in the lives of the people you care about, and in the world in general! The possibilities are limitless!

Life is a journey . . . one step at a time. You're taking your first steps up an exciting, dynamic path . . . one that will take you into great adventures and experiences! Embrace these first steps . . . as a wonderful beginning of a new, amazing life!

Now let's begin the journey . . .

I-LIGNMENT STEP 1:

Shift Your Perspective
(First Shift of Transformation)

A shift in perspective is critical for your transformation. Without it, authentic transformation cannot occur. The following activities have been designed to aid in this powerful shift during I-Lignment.

> NOTE: *Two symbols will be used throughout the process. The first, is a book symbol* 📖 *. This points you to sections of the book that are important to that part of the I-Lignment process. The second symbol is the footprint symbol* 👣 *. This indicates an action you need to take as part of your transformational journey.*

To shift your perspective, play full out and do all of the following . . .

📖 Read the "ILignment" Book

You've hopefully already read the book to this point and made a major shift in your perspective. If you haven't already, please go back and read the prior chapters in full and in the order presented for greatest impact.

📖 Review Book Chapters/Sections . . . during the I-Lignment Process

As mentioned, during "Your Transformation Journey," you'll be referred to some of the chapters and sections of the book to review to reinforce your new perspective and aid in your transformation with information relevant to that point in the process.

ᘓᔆ Sign up for "Freer Journey" Weekly Blog

Weekly email messages will be sent out to empower you on your I-Lignment journey and to reinforce many of the concepts as they apply to different parts of your life.

Sign up at FreerJourney.com/home at the bottom of the web page.

I-LIGNMENT STEP 2:

Empower Your Journey

Just like for any new trip, it's best experienced if you're pre-pared for the journey. If you don't prepare, it can negatively impact the quality of your experience and decrease your chances of reaching the goal . . . your Greatest Life.

Here's a list of the ways you can be best positioned . . .

૮ૐ Make This Your Own Journey

This is critically important! So far, your life has been largely manufactured by others, outside-in. As you go through I-Lign-ment, you need to reverse your old way of life and make your transformation your own, inside-out. No one can do the transformation for you; you need to do it for yourself. It's an inside job . . . if you want your new life to be authentic. Even if you're working with a professional coach or counselor, they should only help you with the process. The inner change and creating your new life can be done only by you; you don't want to let anyone hijack the process of creating the new you!

It's important to understand you can continue to live your life in a giving, loving way. It's the inner transformation that needs to be "selfishly" done with no outer influences. Afterward, you'll have the rest of your life to give to others "selflessly" as you live your new life of purpose and possibility in service of others!

૮ૐ Start Right Where You Are . . . It's the Perfect (and Only) "Time"

Right now is absolutely the best time to start . . . no matter your current life circumstances. It's so common for people to procrastinate, waiting for all the conditions to be perfect before they start sometime in the future. Don't make that mistake. Start now! You'll never find a better time. In fact, it's the only time to start, since the present moment is the only time there is. It's where all your power lies to make anything happen.

Never ever think it's too late in your life to start. Right now, today, is the most important day of your life. Move forward boldly and with passion. It can be the beginning of a phenomenal life that unfolds quickly.

Location doesn't matter either. Trying to go somewhere special to transform is just added drama that keeps you stuck. Right where you are, right now, is the perfect place to start. Say to yourself, "I AM transforming my life now." Feel the power of that committed and definitive decision. Repeat this to yourself daily.

👣 Go at Your Own Pace

This isn't a race in competition with others. This is your journey; you get to determine the pace. Therefore, you need not be concerned with anyone else's opinion regarding your progress or deadlines, nor do you need to compare yourself with anyone else. Your transformation is unique to you, and how you progress is up to you as well. There are no time frames for any of the following I-Lignment process steps. You'll know intuitively when you need to move from one step to the next. Once you do, if you feel like you need to take a step back to a prior step and move forward through the process again from that point on, do so. Again, intuitively, you'll know the right pace for you and whether you've completed the step.

✦ Create Your Space

Find a quiet spot that you can consistently go to during the morning and evening Empowering the "I"ntersection" meditation periods. By having this special space, you create a consistent routine that separates you from everyday life, allowing you to go deep without interruption.

Some people have that space in their own homes, especially if they live alone or with an understanding partner or housemate. If you have young kids, it can be much more challenging to do it in your home. If a space in your house is not an option, there are many other possibilities. Some people retreat to their RVs or an outbuilding on their property. Some find a quiet corner in a coffee shop, hotel lobby, or library. Others incorporate it with their morning and evening outdoor exercise routine by spending time in a secluded section of a park.

I've found my car to be an effective place for transformation. To and from work, you can find an inspirational spot to spend time. Or, if you work from home, you can jump in the car and drive to a quiet spot in the morning and evening. If you want complete privacy, you can buy window shades for the front and side car windows to create a completely secluded spot instantly, no matter where you are.

Whatever space you find that works for you, what's most important is having a committed consistency of location and time so you don't let logistics and life get in the way of your inner work.

✦ Create Your Daily Routine ... for Empowering the "I"ntersection

It's important you create a routine that empowers your transformational journey. As you know, the only place and time transformation will occur is in each new present moment.

The routine creates the conditions for this real transformation to occur . . . every day . . . naturally.

To help you create your daily routine . . .

⬜ Review the section "I-Ligned Life . . . in Each Moment" on page 147.

As mentioned, the use and emphasis of the Empowering the "I"ntersection daily routine will change along your I-Lignment journey.

> *"At first, it'll be used to empower you as you journey inward to your "I"ntersection . . . your authentic "I." Then it will shift to empower you to create a life from the inside-out . . . uncovering your innermost, authentic intentions. Last, it will become a way of life, in each moment, as you bring your inner intentions to reality."*

It's important to keep the structure of your daily routine the same throughout I-Lignment and change only one area of the routine along the way: your intentions.

At the start of I-Lignment, your intentions will be twofold. First, you'll be committed to your inward journey with the intent of living in and from your authentic "I" . . . accomplished through daily meditation and release. Second, you'll have an interim Dynamic Possibility and plan you're pursuing. Even though, most likely, the current possibility and plan will not ultimately be in alignment with your True Purpose, it's important to continue to live your life in service of others as you go through transformation.

Once you reach your "I"ntersection and shift the source of your life to your Inner Source, you're now intent on creating a new, authentic life created from the inside-out through the discovery of a whole new set of intentions . . . Inner Purpose, Dynamic Possibility with your I-Ligned Life Plan, "I" FEEL, and "I" AM.

Last, once your inner intentions are discovered, you'll bring them to reality through a concentrated focus on them at the beginning of each day as part of your routine.

Staying consistent with your daily routine cannot be emphasized enough. It's the only way to accelerate the journey to your Greatest Life.

Stay Open and Focused on the Journey . . . Not a Specific Destination

I-Lignment is a transformational process to journey to and then live your Greatest Life from your authentic "I." It's changing your way of living life at the core. Once you do, it becomes a way of life. It becomes a lifelong journey . . . and beyond.

Trust the process! Don't focus on a specific outcome but rather allow the outcome to naturally unfold. Life is okay at each point during this transformation. Know that all is well and going according to the way it should be. When you do this, you open yourself to unlimited possibilities along the way . . . both in terms of your inner transformation as well as the new life you're creating.

Get rid of expectations. It's in the discovery of what we don't know that real, powerful personal growth occurs.

Trusting the process also allows you to continue down the path of transformation, without giving up, when you feel weak, afraid, uncertain, and confused. In those moments, you can just trust in the process and continue your journey.

👣 Avoid Anything that Inhibits Awareness of Your Emotions

We've developed all sorts of ways to deal with our negative emotions and thoughts. Most of them fall into one of two buckets: we cover them up or run away from them. By doing either of these, you're not setting yourself up to see the emotions when they arise, hear the message, and release them. You need to create the conditions to be fully aware of your emotions, beliefs, words, actions, and the reactions of others if you want to see/feel life as it is and to eliminate the internal blocks that hinder the flow of life from within.

It is, therefore, recommended during I-Lignment to significantly reduce or stop anything that dampens the ability to be fully aware, especially alcohol and drugs.

You also need to avoid making any physical changes in your life, such as moving someplace else or altering your physical appearance. Any of these tactics are, in essence, running from what's happening in your life right here, right now. These types of activities add only drama to your life and take time away from your inner transformation work.

👣 Take 100 Percent Responsibility for Your Life Experience

You can't transform your life if you think you're a victim of the world. If you do, the world out there and the people in it need to change before you can, and most of them won't. Even worse, when you blame others for your life situation, you give away your power to them. You truly become a powerless victim.

The truth: You are responsible for 100 percent (not 95 percent or 99 percent but 100 percent) of your emotions, thoughts, beliefs, stories, words, and actions. Every one of them comes from within you. You, in reality, have the Inner

Power to choose whether you have/do them or not. It's just that you're not using that power.

Most people don't realize this because their emotions, thoughts, beliefs, and stories are being triggered by people and events around them. It appears they're being impacted by things "out there," but it's what is in them that is the real cause of the reaction.

As you begin to take 100 percent responsibility, you'll start to realize that many of the experiences you're having in life are the result of how you're showing up in the world and in the lives of others. You'll realize that the emotional energy you emit, the thoughts you have, the words you speak, and the actions you take are creating many of the life experiences you're having. Their current source is your own shell . . . your inauthentic "i."

This concept of taking 100 percent responsibility for everything in your life is a key element of your transformation. With this understanding and responsibility, you then can effectively go inward to the real source of all your inhibiting experiences and reactions in life and get rid of the underlying causes for good. Take 100 percent responsibility for all your experiences on your transformational journey. Take on the powerful belief, "Life is happening for me, not to me."

✺ Be Kind to Yourself

As you go through transformation and are experiencing your negative emotional charges, it's easy to fall into the trap of beating yourself up for the past. Don't do it! Remember, the past is gone and no longer exists. The only reality is right now, where you can make different choices in each new present moment.

Be kind to yourself during the transformation process and beyond. Our "Inner Power" gives us the strength to do this! Remember, at your core is unconditional love. Unconditionally love yourself and be at peace with where you are right now. You are exactly where you need to be on your life's journey.

Be kind to yourself . . . always!

👣 Commit . . . Don't Just Try

There's a huge difference between "trying" to do something and being committed to doing it.

Trying is weak; committed is strong. Trying decreases the odds of accomplishing your goals; being committed increases significantly your odds of being successful. Trying is half-hearted; committed is full out. Trying gives you an escape route if things aren't going according to plan; committed burns all bridges of escape.

Be fully committed to your personal transformation journey and the I-Lignment process. Be firm on your goal of creating a new possibility in your life, not sliding back into past ways of being based on fear or the expectations of others.

Be fully committed to your own unique, individual journey. Stay true to this course. Recommit every day through the Empowering the "I"ntersection routine. Be committed and take the right massive action to make it happen. Don't think of failure, only success, and that you are committed to continuing the effort until you have gotten it done.

Commit . . . commit . . . commit!

I-LIGNMENT STEP 3:

Ask: Where am "i"?

"The unexamined life is not worth living."
—SOCRATES

You have greatness within you; it's always been there. You've always had the ability to experience deep peace and have all the unconditional love you want. Your individual freedom is an inherent right. You've always had infinite possibilities available to you. You've always had the potential to realize your Greatest Life.

What's stopped you?

You know what that answer is now . . . it's your inauthentic self "i." You've been lost in the fog of your shell, separated from who you really are. You haven't been able to see the greatness that has been lying dormant in you, waiting to be rediscovered.

Isn't it about time to really understand what stands in your way? The starting point for a real personal transformation is an honest, sincere examination of your life.

Let's start this exploration . . .

📖 Review Chapter Two: "Why? Why Is My Life Like This?" . . .

👣 Have a pen and notebook ready as you reread the chapter. When something comes up that you believe is holding you back from realizing your Greatest Life, write it down immediately. Also, look for answers to the questions below as you read the chapter. Once you're done reading the chapter, continue to answer the questions until you feel you've addressed them as best as you can.

- What pushes my buttons? What emotions and thoughts come up when they get pushed? How do I react?
- What are my strongest disempowering emotions? What are the underlying causes of those emotions? (See Appendix A for a list of common emotions.)
- What limiting beliefs do I have? What are the strongest limiting beliefs? What are my top three? (See Appendix A for a list of common limiting beliefs.)
- What are my "wants" from life? (See Appendix A for a list of common wants.)
- How do I try to cover up or subdue uncomfortable feelings, emotions, and thoughts?
- What are my disempowering habits? What are the underlying causes of these habits?
- What are the dominant, disempowering "stories" in my life?
- How am I being a victim?
- What identity have I created that's holding me back?
- What expectations do other people have about my life that are holding me back?
- What challenging relationships do I have? What makes them a challenge?
- What impact are these things having on my life right now? What are causing the biggest impact?

When you've completed this part of the examination of your life, now . . .

👣 Rate Yourself on "The Transformed You" Assessment in Appendix B.

This initial "The Transformed You" assessment reveals how disempowering living in and from your shell can be. On average, the ratings in most categories tend to be in the mid to low range.

Write down any additional insights you have as you're doing the assessment in terms of what's blocking you from realizing your Greatest Life.

Also write down how you'd like to be living life differently. Explore these additional questions:

- How would I like my life to be different in each of the following areas of my life: Emotionally? Mentally? Physically? Relationships? Work? Financially? Adventure?
- What do I love to do? What would I be doing whether I got paid for it or not?
- What group of people in the world would I love to serve and bring more value into their lives? Why?
- What are my strengths?
- What are my skills?
- What's going right in my life?
- What areas in my life, if I changed, would make the biggest difference?

Keep your self-examination notes handy for use later in the I-Lignment process.

I-LIGNMENT STEP 4:

Create Motivation . . . the "Big Why"

To achieve any big change in your life, you need to have a big enough "why." Without it, the sheer momentum of your inauthentic life, coupled with your own fears associated with change and the influence of people around you interested in maintaining the status quo, keeps you stuck . . . traveling down the Grand Canyon of life in one predetermined direction.

There's an important concept that lays the groundwork for the discovery of your Big Why. It's the concept of Pain–Gain. People will go to great lengths to avoid pain and will do the same to gain something in their life that gives them feelings of pleasure and achieving something much grander than what they have. So if you want to create powerful motivation to initiate and achieve changes in your life, you need to associate massive pain with staying the same and associate massive pleasure and gain with changing to an alternative way of living life. To create the greatest motivation for change, you need to do both. The pain will push you to action . . . and the pleasurable gain will pull you to action.

CREATING THE TWO PARTS OF YOUR BIG WHY

👣 **Part One: Create Massive "Pain":** There's a reason you're reading this book. Your life isn't great right now. Why is that? Go back and review your notes and answers to the questions in the last I-Lignment step. Really "see"

252

the dysfunction that has you stuck in an unacceptable life. Feel the pain from living this type of life. Realize how you have been negatively impacted in the past and present. See how you've been hurting the people you love. Feel it deeply. Experience the pain with all your senses . . . see it, feel it, hear it, smell it, taste it. Look forward five years in the future. See it continuing to have the same or worse impact on your life. See it impacting how you see yourself and how others see you. Think about everything you have lost by living this way. Imagine even more pain inflicted on yourself and the people you care about. Then project it out even further . . . ten years . . . twenty years . . . and go through the same process. See your quality of life continuing to painfully deteriorate.

Do you really want to continue to live this way? Do you want to continue to have this pain?

Shout . . . Nooooooo!

👣 Part Two: Envision a Life of Great Pleasurable "Gain."

Envision the life you've always dreamed about.

📖 **Review Chapter Ten: "The Transformed You"!** Use this review to give you ideas of the type of life you could be living.

Spend quality time developing this vision of your new, beautiful life. Allow this vision to flow from deep inside you; allow it to unfold from the inside-out.

Once complete, put yourself into it as if it's happening right now. See it, feel it, hear it, smell it, taste it. Your relationships are loving and harmonious. Your life's work is in synch with every other part of your life. You're filled to the brim with unconditional love. You have a deep inner peace that is unshakable. You feel a freedom you've never felt before

. . . a freedom to live a life of your choosing. You have a deep sense of joy always. You're grateful for what life is bringing your way. You feel you're contributing to others and making a powerful, positive difference in the world.

Shout **"Yes"** to this new, powerful, beautiful life.

You're now empowered with the **Big Why** . . . you clearly see what is unacceptable in your life . . . and you also have a clear picture of an amazing life that will replace it.

👣 If it helps, create a large storyboard with pictures representing your current life at the bottom of the board and the amazing life you desire at the top. Right in the middle of the storyboard, put an arrow that points up. Write on the arrow, "I'm Committed to Achieving an Amazing Life." Put the storyboard where you can see it every day.

I-LIGNMENT STEP 5:
Create an Interim Dynamic Possibility and Plan

You don't want to wait until you discover your life's purpose to start living life powerfully in service of others. It's important to create an interim Dynamic Possibility and plan now and live it while you're going through your transformation. If you're lucky, it'll be in total alignment with your ultimate True Purpose, but, most likely, you'll need to make changes once your Inner Purpose is realized.

📖 *Review the section "Dynamic Possibility" on page 131.*

This section was written as if you've already discovered your life's purpose. Understand this as you read it. It still will allow you to create the interim Dynamic Possibility and plan . . . and will also reinforce the same approach required to create your Dynamic Possibility and I-Ligned Life Plan once your life's purpose is revealed.

👣 Now create your interim Dynamic Possibility and plan. It's powerful to go off by yourself somewhere inspirational for a minimum three-day retreat to allow yourself to focus, reflect, and be creative.

I-LIGNMENT STEP 6:

Journey to "I"
(Second Shift of Transformation . . . Shift of Source)

📖 **Review Chapter Eight: "Journey to the "I"ntersection introduction"!**

BE PRESENT . . . NOW

📖 **Review Chapter Eight, Section "Be Present . . . Now"!**
There are two ways you will practice "being present."

👣 The first is through the formal practice of being present

during the meditations in the morning and then evenings as part of Empowering the "I"ntersection.

To help you become proficient at this practice, there's an I-Lignment meditation, "Be Present," in Appendix C, "I-Lignment Meditation and Release Techniques." The meditation is provided in both written format in the appendix and coach-guided audio format at FreerJourney.com/Be-Present. Before you do the "Be Present" meditation, first read the introduction in Appendix C, which describes the concept and purpose of meditation and release.

👣 The second practice is through being present throughout the day with something present with you in that moment. Focusing on something you see, smell, hear, touch, or taste brings you into the present moment instantly.

Be consistent in practicing these two ways of being present daily. By doing so, you'll create a habit that will empower your transformation and will evolve into a powerful way of life . . . being present in every moment!

INCREASE BODY/EMOTIONS/MIND AWARENESS

📖 **Review Chapter Eight, Section "Body/Emotions/Mind Awareness"!**

👣 To develop your ability to fully experience and be aware of your body and the inner emotional and mental makeup, there is an I-Lignment meditation, "Be Present to Inner Awareness," in Appendix C, "I-Lignment Meditation and Release Techniques." The meditation is provided in both written format in the appendix and coach-guided audio format at FreerJourney.com/Inner-Awareness.

At the beginning of I-Lignment, it's important to find many periods when you can get present and increase your awareness of your body sensations, emotions, thoughts, beliefs, and stories. This awareness is critical to be effective at revealing the contents of your shell, "seeing" the impact of it all on your life, uncovering the underlying cause, and then in the releasing or dissolving of your shell.

Keep working at increasing this awareness until you're able to go into your body when you're experiencing unease, then quickly feel and understand what emotions and beliefs are coming to the surface, where they're being felt in the body, and with what intensity.

CREATE SEPARATION... GOING BEYOND YOUR SHELL

Review Chapter Eight, Section "Creating Separation"!

To experience this separation, there's an I-Lignment meditation, "Be Present to Your True Self," in Appendix C, "I-Lignment Meditation and Release Techniques." The meditation is provided in both written format in the appendix and coach-guided audio format at FreerJourney.com/True-Self.

If you continue to believe who you are is your shell (your body, your inner emotions and beliefs, your existing behaviors, your appearance, and your life experiences), any suggestion you need to get rid of your shell to discover the real you that lies beyond it is met with stiff inner resistance. It's why this meditation is so important. It allows you to experience, through a gentle process, the real you separate from the shell. Once you experience the real you, you become an external observer of what is going on within your shell. Being separate allows you to be okay with anything you see in your shell, no matter how dysfunctional, because you know it isn't the real you. You'll increasingly be willing to let go of the shell bit by bit as the emotions and beliefs come up to be heard and then released.

Keep using the meditation until you're fully experiencing your true self as an external, neutral observer of your current life, with a knowing that this is who you are in truth . . . not your inauthentic shell.

DISSOLVE THE SHELL

📖 **Review Chapter Eight, Section "Dissolving the Shell"!**

Now begins your "uncovery." This is such an important part of I-Lignment and your journey to your Greatest Life. Unless you're able to dissipate your shell and discover your authentic "I" that lies beyond it, you'll not have the true "I"ndividual freedom to create your new life from the inside-out.

👣 Go to Appendix C, "I-Lignment Meditation and Release Techniques," and become familiar with each of the four release techniques overall. Then start with the first one, "i-Release," and use it as you get triggered throughout the day and when inhibiting emotions/beliefs surface during the formal meditation and release sessions. This first technique is powerful because it's so easy to use in any situation to release in the moment. It's one you need to learn well and keep in your back pocket for use anytime . . . for the rest of your life.

As you get proficient with the first technique and are experiencing success releasing, begin to try the other three techniques one at a time. Once you've tried them all, pick the ones that work best for you.

It's important to emphasize that "dissolving the shell" isn't something you do overnight. It's a sustainable process of allowing everyday life to bring up the elements of your shell (emotions, beliefs, wants) that need to be seen, heard, and released in that moment. Don't overcomplicate this or think all issues need to be heard and released immediately. The issues will come into your awareness, typically by getting triggered by a person, event, or object, at the right time for the right reasons. Let it happen naturally.

If this is done consistently and consciously, your shell is thinned piece by piece. It's a gentler process this way rather than trying to dredge up all the negative in your life over a weekend to release all at once.

By the inch, it's a cinch.
By the yard, it's hard.

If you've created an Empowering the "I"ntersection routine, that includes meditation and release, and you've committed to doing it consistently daily, then dissipating your shell is inevitable and reaching your authentic "I" will become a reality.

NOTE: If you're having a difficult time identifying what's going on within you as you're going through meditation and release or at any other time, you can refer to the lists of common emotions, beliefs, and needs in Appendix A. In addition, you can access help through individual or group coaching by visiting FreerJourney.com/I-Lignment.

👣 To begin dissolving the shell, you can go back to your notes from the discovery work you did in "Where am 'i'?" Take one thing that is still impacting your life right now to release. Don't pick one of the major issues to start; pick one that's moderately impacting you. You want experience having it released; picking an issue that is less emotionally charged makes this experience easier. Use the first release technique, "i-Release," on it until you feel it greatly reduced in intensity or completely gone . . . leaving a feeling of peace and spaciousness where there was before a negative intensity and denseness.

👣 Repeat this on the other inhibiting emotions and beliefs uncovered during "Where am 'i'?"

👣 Then continue to use the release techniques as more inhibiting emotions/beliefs arise in your daily life. Keep doing this every day until you strip away all the layers that have been built up over the years to expose only what is real . . . the real you . . . "I."

SHIFT YOUR SOURCE OF LIFE (Second Shift of Transformation)

📖 Review Chapter Eight, Section, "Shift of Source"!

👣 Cultivate your ability to hear your Inner Voice by

consistently doing the morning meditation and intentionally opening up to hear Inner Guidance for the day. Also, take those opportunities throughout the day when you know you need to stop and listen for guidance. Get quiet and calm . . . and listen. Trust and take right action on what you hear . . . as long as it's coming from a place of unconditional love, deep peace, and true freedom for you and others.

By doing this, you'll increasingly be living your life inside-out . . . from an Inner Source of unlimited possibility!

I-LIGNMENT STEP 7:

Create Your Greatest Life . . . from "I"
(Third Shift of Transformation . . . Shift of Intention)

You're now at a powerful place in your transformation to create the life you've always dreamed of!

📖 **Review Chapter Nine: "Living Your Greatest Life . . . from 'I'" introduction!**

BE IN "FLOW" . . . FROM WITHIN

📖 **Review Chapter Nine, Section "Be in the 'Flow' . . . from Within"!**

👣 Increase the times throughout the day when you consciously stop and listen internally for guidance. Know your ultimate goal is to become a master at being able to hear your Inner Guidance in any moment and take action on that guidance in complete trust . . . with a "knowing" that it's the right thing to do.

When you're able to do this in each moment, then you're truly in the flow of life from within . . . living life from the inside-out.

Always go inward for your guidance first . . . trust in that guidance . . . and act on that guidance.

DISCOVER YOUR LIFE'S PURPOSE

📖 **Review Chapter Nine, Section "Uncovering Your Life's Purpose"!**

👣 When you ask the open-ended question during meditation, "What is my life purpose?" you're opening yourself up to any possibility from an unlimited source. I used to call this process "brainstorming" but realized this approach implied a reliance on the limited mind. I now call it "allowing infinite intelligence." It better describes the deep connection you're establishing with the infinite source of possibilities.

Keep asking the question, "What is my life purpose?" every day until it reveals itself! Trust that it will at the right time!

When you discover your purpose, it will feel intuitively right. It'll make you feel like jumping out of bed in the morning to do it . . . whether you got paid to do it or not. It'll also have an outward focus on serving others in some powerful way.

CREATE YOUR DYNAMIC POSSIBILITY AND I-LIGNED LIFE PLAN

📖 Review Chapter Nine, Section "Dynamic Possibility"!

👣 Set a date for a three-day to one-week personal retreat to create your Dynamic Possibility and I-Ligned Life Plan following the planning process shown in the "Dynamic Possibility" section of the book.

UNCOVER "I" FEEL AND "I" AM

📖 Review Chapter Nine, Section "Intentions"!

👣 Create your "I" FEEL _____ list. Imagine that you are living your Dynamic Possibility right now. Envision it with all your senses . . . see it, hear it, touch it, smell it, be emotional about it. While you're fully in the vision of your possibility, write down the way you're feeling. Complete the sentence, "I" FEEL _____ (fill in the blank). Come up with as many feelings as you can.

👣 Create your "I" AM _____ list. While you're still in the possibility, write down all the ways you'll be showing up in life. Complete the sentence, "I" AM _____ (fill in the blank). Come up with as many ways you're showing up in life as you can.

AUTHENTIC CONNECTION WITH OTHERS

📖 **Review Chapter Nine, Section "Authentic Connection with Others"!**

There are four things you need to do to empower the relationships in your life.

👣 First, look at all your current relationships differently. Begin by bringing your new ways of interacting with others and your new abilities that are made possible from living a life in and from "I" into the relationships most important to you. Where you have issues in a relationship, focus on using the I-Lignment release technique "I-Forgive" to let go of whatever is creating the block between you and the other person. Intentionally do this for at least one person daily during the morning meditation and release period. Observe how the relationships change. In most cases, they will significantly improve as you begin interacting with them "I" to "I" . . . coming from a place of unconditional love.

👣 Second, make your "I"ntentions visible to the world around you . . . with your family, friends, coworkers, and acquaintances; on social media; with people you meet on the street; and with anyone else you think appropriate. Broadcast the new you to the Universe! Start the magnetic attraction of the right relationships into your life.

👣 Third, watch the reaction of your current relationships to the announcement of your new "I"ntentions. Do they support you or do they try to tear you down and throw up blocks? Their response will determine the type of relationship you have with them moving forward. Determine if you're going to spend more or less time with that person . . . or if it's a relationship you no longer want in your life.

𝕗 Fourth, pay attention to new relationships that are being attracted into your life in support of your "I"ntentions. Don't miss the opportunities . . . especially those that are not apparent. Sometimes they show up in unexpected ways or in ways that are subtle.

By doing these four things, you'll build a powerful, supportive group of people who will be a big reason your "I"ntentions become a reality. It'll be the amazing group of people you share your Greatest Life with!

ASSESS THE AUTHENTIC YOU . . . "I"

When you started your transformation journey, you rated yourself on "The Transformed You" assessment. It's good to go back periodically and take the assessment again to see where you are.

𝕗 Re-Rate Yourself on "The Transformed You" Scales in Appendix B. When you do, indicate this is the second time you have assessed yourself so you can see your progress. Each time you reassess, mark it differently.

Once completed, look at the overall progress you've made. Also, look at each specific area to see how you've been progressing.

REPEAT THE I-LIGNMENT PROCESS . . . IF NECESSARY

👣 If there are areas in "The Transformed You . . . Scales to Measure Progress" assessment that show additional inner work needs to be done, then repeat the I-Lignment process again, starting at Step 3.

I-LIGNMENT STEP 8:

Create a New World

📖 **Review Chapter Twelve: "Change Your World . . . Change The World"!**

You're now empowered to "Change the World" in multiple ways!

The "transformed you" will have a great influence on all you touch in your daily life! Your presence and how you're serving the world will ripple into the lives of others . . . influencing their lives directly. It will then ripple through them into the lives of the people they touch as well!

You'll also be a catalyst for others to transform into their Greatest Life. As they interact with you, they'll reflect on how they're living life themselves and see there's a better way. They'll see, through your example of what's possible, that they, too, have a path to realize their Greatest Life!

As you join forces with a growing group of people living in and from their authentic "I," the combined energy of the states inherent at "I"— unconditional love, deep peace, true individual freedom, contentment, and joy—will have a growing influence on the world. Others will see there's a better way to live life together and how they, too, can bring their purpose and possibility to serve the world.

 Join the "Change Your World . . . Change the World" movement! Be part of transforming the world!
Go to FreerJourney.com/The-Movement.

Together we can transform our world into a beautiful place!

I-LIGNMENT STEP:

∞

Congratulations! You're now living your Greatest Life . . . that has no end!

Your authentic life is one of purpose, unlimited possibility, adventure, and many exciting experiences ... lived now. Your abundant world is providing resources to enable you to bring your unique gift to the world in the service of others. You're sharing this journey with a growing number of people who share a deep connection with you "I" to "I" . . . and who, too, are bringing their unique gift to the world.

Unconditional Love is at the core of everything you do and is the solid foundation for your entire life.

You have finally arrived . . .

"I" . . . Authentic You Forever!

Love Always ♥
–Ron

APPENDIX

APPENDIX A:
LISTS ... FOR YOUR
TRANSFORMATION

THE FOLLOWING ARE lists of common examples of emotions, beliefs, and wants to aid you in your I-Lignment journey. You can refer to these lists as you do your own self-assessment or when you're having trouble identifying what's being triggered in your life.

The inability to identify specific emotions is common for many of us because of our detachment from our emotions. This list is intended to help break through this barrier.

As you identify and release on the inhibiting/lower-energy/lower-consciousness emotions, beliefs, and wants, you'll be dissipating the shell and moving inward to the empowering/higher-energy/higher-consciousness emotions and beliefs that are inherent at your core . . . at your authentic "I."

EMOTIONS & BELIEFS

Shell = "i"
Inhibiting Emotions & Beliefs
Lower Energy
Lower Consciousness
Limited Individual Freedom

"I"ntersection = "I"
Empowering Emotions & Beliefs
Higher Energy
Higher Consciousness
True "I"ndividual Freedom

∧

Emotions

Depressed	Grief	Fear	Angry	Wanting	Proud	Willing	Gratitude	Love	Peace
Confused	Let down	Anxious	Pissed off	Something's missing	Accomplished	Inner Clarity	All is well	Unconditional	Inner quiet
Overwhelmed	Abandoned	Cautious	Outraged	Acquiring	I've won	Inspired	Present	In Presence	Timeless
Paralyzed	Deceived	Distrustful	Vindictive	Always need more	I have more	Empowered	Abundance	Deep Connection	Centered
Powerless	Manipulated	Threatened	Upset	Driven	Special	Purpose	Aware	Commitment	Whole
Messed up	What if?	Attacked	Irate	Craving	Intellectually superior	Courage to change	Open	Steadfast	Presence
Hopeless	Regretful	Panic	Lashing out	Selfish	Critical	Initiative	Receptive	Purity of motive	Inner light
All Alone	Unloved	Fear of being alone	Annoyed	Envious	Judgmental	Daring	Accepting	Generous	Oneness
Unworthy	Unlovable	Fear of criticism	Betrayed	Greedy	Arrogant	Powerful	Embracing	Kindness	Authentic
Invisible	Guilty	Fear or Rejection	Indignant	Calculating	Always right	Passionate	Appreciative	Affection	Spacious
Empty	Sorry	Fear of failure	Attacking	Clingy	Boastful	Energetic	You're okay	Caring	True Freedom
Worthless	Abused	Fear of death	Wrathful	Possessive	Righteous	Open	Kind	Warmth	Unlimited
No energy	Cheated		Revengeful	Jealous	Unforgiving	Creative	Natural	Forgiving	Fulfilled
Lost	Dejected		Destructive	Self-absorbed	Closed off	Capable	Harmonious	Nurturing	Content
Deadened	Heartbroken		Justified	Impatient	Isolated	Resourceful	In Flow	Content	Joy
Joyless	Left behind		Mean	Pushy	Empty inside	Focused	Radiant	Uplifted	Perfection
Worthless	Longing		Violent			Resilient	Joyful	Protective	Absence of negativity
Giving up	Unwanted		Don't care						
<-----	<-----	<----	<-----	<-----	<-----	<-----	<-----	<-----	<-----

I suck. I'll never succeed. I'm a failure. I can't do it. I can't win. I don't care. I don't matter. I'll never get over this. I'm a failure. I'm a fraud. I'm an imposter. I'm a victim. I'm too old. I'm too tired. I'm too young. I'm not worthy of attention.

I'm alone. Nobody loves me. Nobody cares. I'm not lovable. People will never understand the real me. I'll never find love in my life. There are no more good fish in the sea. Love is too hard to find. I might as well give up. There is no time to think about my health. If only ...

I'm a failure. They'll think I'm stupid. I don't have enough education. I don't know the right people. I need someone else to succeed. If I move, I'll be happy. I'll never find a job I love. I'm an imposter. I'm not good enough. The world is dangerous. There's so much to be angry about.

Revenge will settle the score. I'll never forgive them. Hurting them will make things right. They're the enemy. It was their fault. They don't deserve forgiveness. I'm a victim. We must punish them. We need to destroy them. Eye for an eye. War is the only choice.

With him, I'll feel complete. She'll fill the void I feel inside. More money is the answer. Without it, I'm a nobody. With it, I'm a somebody. We live in a world of scarcity. Alcohol will help me cope. Bigger is better. I need to get my slice of the pie. All that matters is I get what I want. For me to win, they need to lose. I'll get it at all costs. It's never enough.

I'm more successful than others. I'm the expert; I know best. I'm better than them. I associate only with the elite. I'm standing my ground at all costs. If I give in, I'll lose. I'm too good for those people. People with college education are smarter. I'll never forgive them for the past. People of my color are better than people of their color.

I can achieve a great life! I can do anything! I'm inches away from success! I'm open and ready for change! I'll do whatever it takes! I'm willing to do the work! I am unstoppable! I am all powerful! I will persevere! I'll find the resources I need.

The world is my oyster! Everything is okay! All is the way it should be! I live in a world of abundance! Life is working for me, not against me! The Universe is conspiring to help me! Everything that happens in my life is for my higher good! Everything that happens to me is a learning opportunity! People are trying their best!

I AM love ... unconditional love! I can be in the "state of love" with infinite people! I have unlimited love to give! I am surrounded by unlimited, unconditional love! Love dissolves hate! Love is an infinite resource! Love lifts all boats! The most important thing in life is love.

A completely authentic life flows only from inner peace! I am always provided for! Inner peace is possible! Outer peace is a reflection of inner peace! True integrity is found only through inner peace! True peace is found within! World peace starts with me!

WANTS

Most wants are from the perception of some lack or scarcity in your life. These perceptions are mostly caused by two things: separation from your authentic self (the existence of the "void" described earlier in the book) and the disempowering makeup of your inauthentic shell. Both create feelings of emptiness (something's missing in your life) and the need to cope. This begins a strong focus on these wants and satisfying them . . . from out there in the world.

However, whatever you focus on, you bring more of it into your life. When you focus on these wants, you tend to bring more of the emptiness, lack, and scarcity into your life. When you, instead, focus on your "I"ntentions, knowing the truth that abundance is all around you, you open yourself up to realizing your "I"ntentions and bringing that abundance into your life.

Thus, releasing on your inhibiting "wants" is critical as you're on the inward journey to your "I"ntersection, as a part of the I-Lignment process. The ultimate release of these wants naturally happens when you're finally living in and from your authentic "I." They dissipate as you experience the attributes of "I" . . . unconditional love, deep peace, true individual freedom, contentment, and joy . . . and as you pursue your authentic "I"ntentions.

The Most Important Inhibiting Wants. Below are the most disempowering wants to release.

Wanting Unconditional Love

As long as you're wanting unconditional love from others, you'll lack it. Unconditional love is rare out in the world; you'll have a tough time finding it out there somewhere. You now know unconditional love exists within you in unlimited supply. When you continue to release wanting unconditional love, you'll soon realize it as you continue to journey inward and begin to live in and from your "I"ntersection . . . your authentic "I." You'll become unconditional love as a natural part of who you are.

Wanting Peace

Trying to find the peace you desire out in the world is tough, especially as you look for it through the lens of your own shell; this peace is increasingly elusive in a world of chaos. You need to let go of wanting peace, knowing the true and deep peace you're looking for already exists when living in and from your "I"ntersection . . . independent of life circumstances and other people.

Wanting Freedom

The desire for personal freedom is strong. You search for it out in the world and look to others to give it to you. As long as you're looking outside yourself to others for your freedom, you'll never find it. True freedom exists only at your "I"ntersection. It's where you have complete freedom to choose your intentions . . . living a purposeful life of your choosing from within. You need to let go of wanting freedom, knowing that true freedom already exists when you're living in and from your "I"ntersection.

Wanting Control

When you're living an outside-in life, you're by and large controlled by others. As a result, you feel a lack of control and, therefore, want and seek control over your life and the world around you. This wanting will never give you control over your life. True control over your destiny exists only when you journey inward to the "I"ntersection of your life and then connect to your Inner Source and follow the guidance you hear. Releasing wanting control will allow you to naturally realize this personal control in a world trying to control you.

Wanting Approval

You've learned to live your life outside-in, seeking guidance outside of yourself for most of what you do. You, therefore, look for the approval from others. Releasing wanting approval will allow you to trust your Inner Voice and create your life from the inside-out. You won't need the approval of others when living an authentic life from your "I"ntersection . . . but you'll get the approval and admiration from many anyway.

Wanting Security

Living in and from your shell is a scary, fearful place (in your mind) where you don't feel like you have a lot of stability in your life. You're buffeted by the multitude of influences over your life, current and past. You also seek consistency in a world out there where change is the only constant. You'll never find the security you want living from this frame of mind. Releasing wanting security and stability out there allows you to flow with life from the inside-out, following your Inner Guidance with a focus on your "I"ntentions . . . trusting that you'll have what you need at the right place and time.

Wanting Separation from Others

Wanting to be separate from others is a result of living from the inauthentic identity of your shell while others do the same. It creates a barrier and results in relating to each other at the surface of life. You'll never discover true, authentic relationships if continuing to live this way. Releasing wanting separation allows you to have deep "I" to "I" relationships and to realize true oneness with others.

Wanting Stuff

An obsession on wanting stuff is a coping mechanism to try to fill the emptiness and lack we feel inside when living in and from our shell. As you're journeying to "I," it's important to understand this and work on releasing the incessant desire to acquire. When you finally dissipate the shell and start fully living an authentic life from "I," you'll be amazed how little you really need to live an amazing life. Simplicity becomes your mantra.

APPENDIX B:

"THE TRANSFORMED YOU"... SCALES TO MEASURE PROGRESS

U SE THE SCALES below to measure your progress along the I-Lignment journey to your Greatest Life. It's recommended you take the assessment at the beginning of the I-Lignment journey and then whenever you want to assess how much progress you've made, as well as to determine what areas of your life to focus on for continued powerful transformation.

If you want a reminder what each of the below descriptions

mean, please go back to the chapter "The Transformed You" on page 187.

You feel whole.

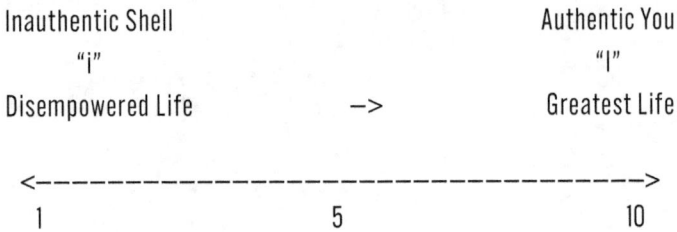

Your newfound freedom is real . . . with unlimited possibilities.

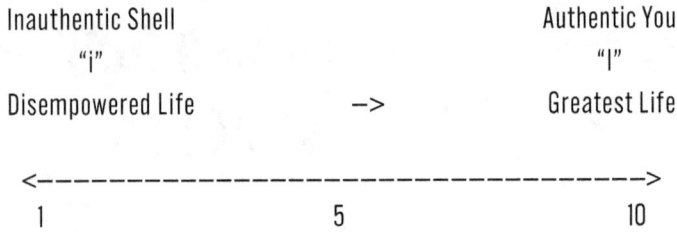

Your life is full of unconditional love . . . independent of anyone else.

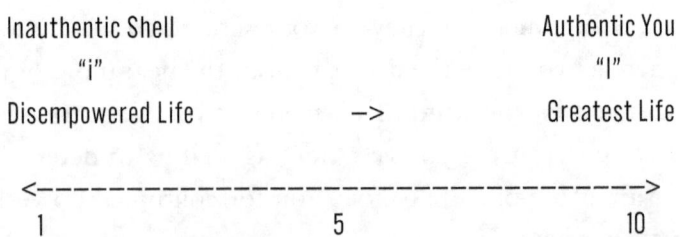

You experience waves of love coming from deep inside you.

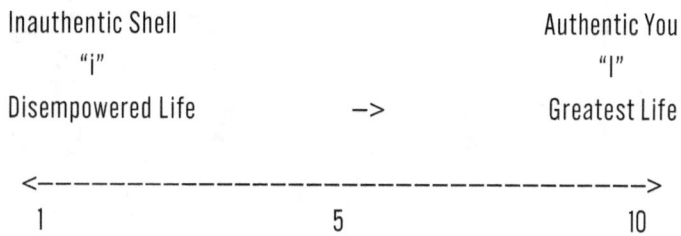

You have a deep sense of peace . . . no matter the circumstances outside of you.

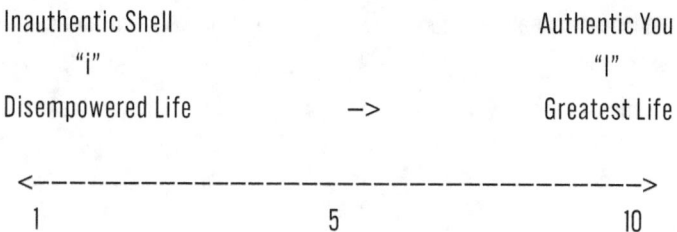

You live life powerfully . . . in each present moment.

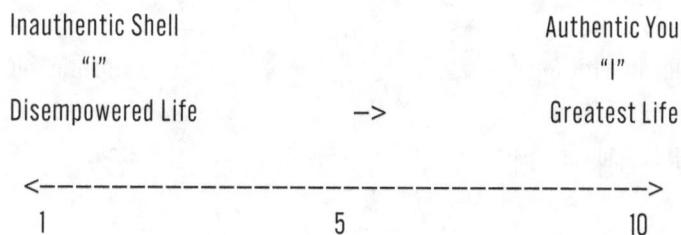

You have a whole new way of being.

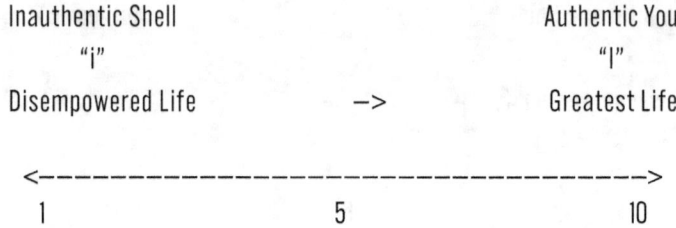

You have found the feelings you want in your life are the feelings inherently felt at your core . . . your authentic "I."

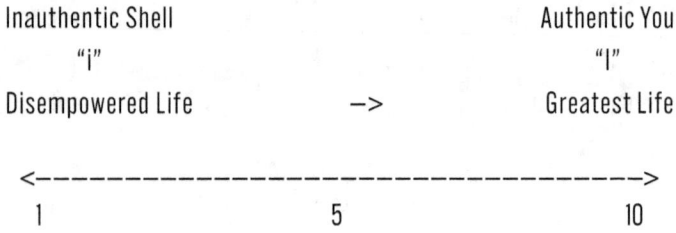

You experience an inner joy that is independent of anything outside of you.

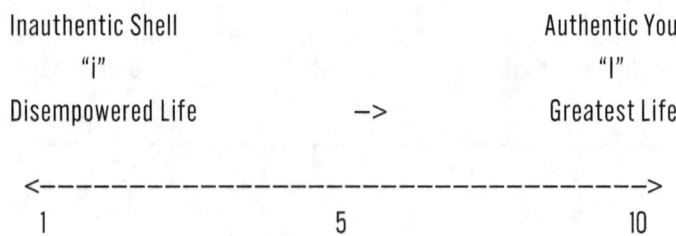

You have a newfound passion for life.

Inauthentic Shell   Authentic You
"¡"   "I"
Disempowered Life   –>   Greatest Life

<--------------------------------------->
1   5   10

You are less impacted by the flow of life outside of you.

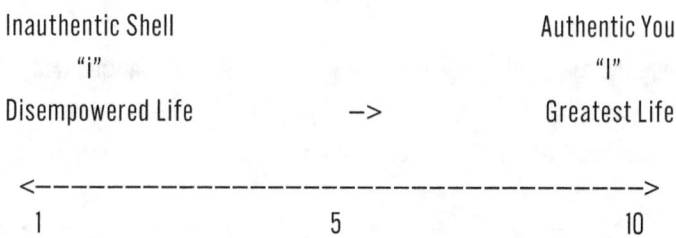

Inauthentic Shell   Authentic You
"¡"   "I"
Disempowered Life   –>   Greatest Life

<--------------------------------------->
1   5   10

Your mind is clear and able to make quicker, better decisions.

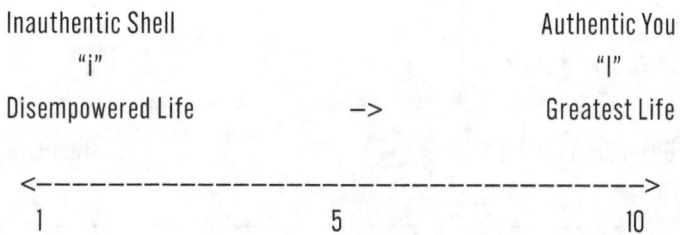

Inauthentic Shell   Authentic You
"¡"   "I"
Disempowered Life   –>   Greatest Life

<--------------------------------------->
1   5   10

You are less reactive to the world around you; rather, you respond based on right actions.

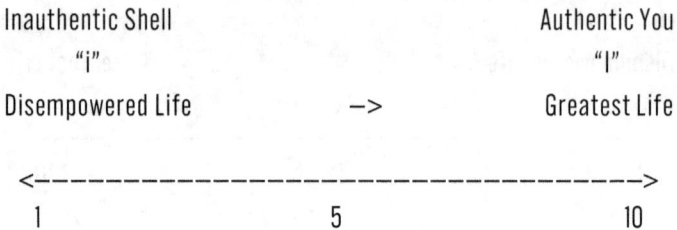

You now know you can handle whatever life throws your way.

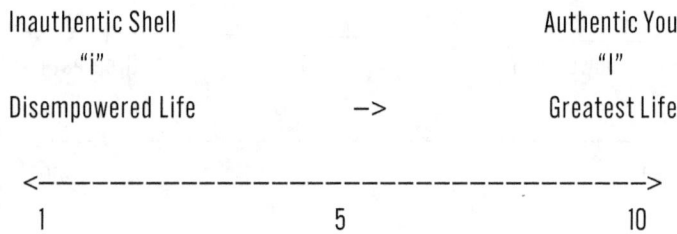

You look at the major events in your life differently.

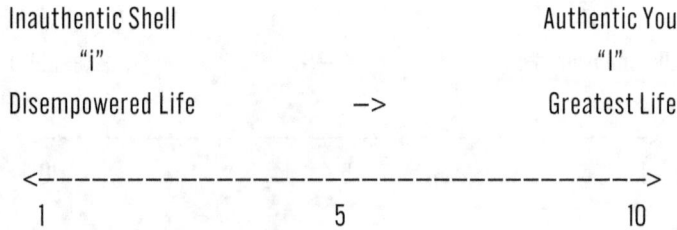

Many of the wants in your life have vanished.

Inauthentic Shell   Authentic You
"i"   "I"
Disempowered Life   ->   Greatest Life

```
<-------------------------------------->
1                    5                   10
```

You are simplifying your life.

Inauthentic Shell   Authentic You
"i"   "I"
Disempowered Life   ->   Greatest Life

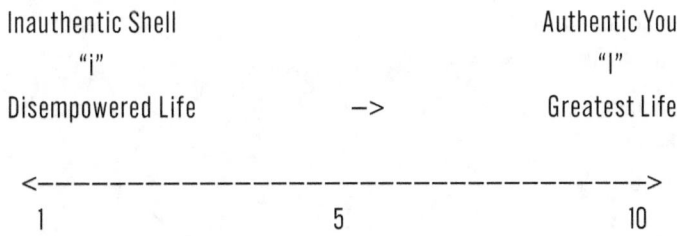

```
<-------------------------------------->
1                    5                   10
```

You have more natural abundance in all parts of your life.

Inauthentic Shell   Authentic You
"i"   "I"
Disempowered Life   ->   Greatest Life

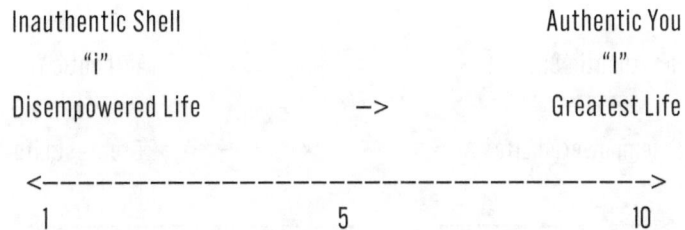

```
<-------------------------------------->
1                    5                   10
```

Your life feels more effortless and enjoyable.

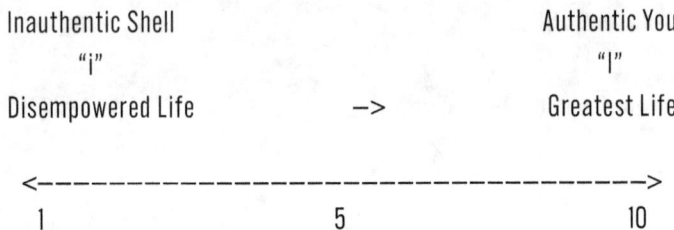

Your relationships are deeper and more authentic.

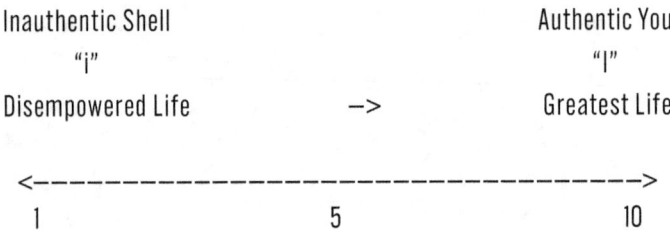

Your experience of falling in love with someone is now powerful and unconditional.

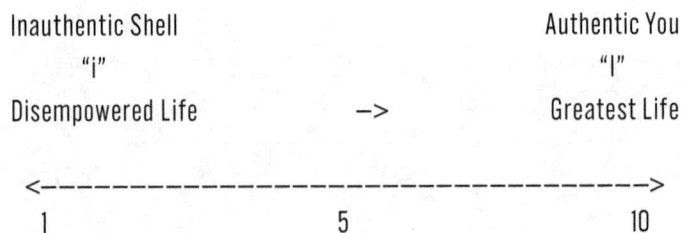

You have become more accepting of others . . . as they are.

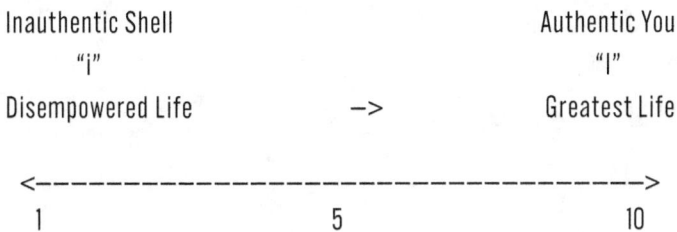

You allow unlimited possibilities for others . . . beyond your own self-interests.

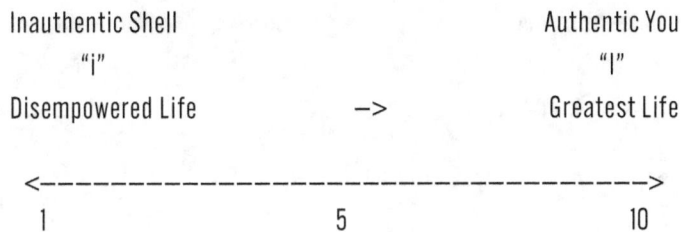

You express many acts of kindness in your daily life.

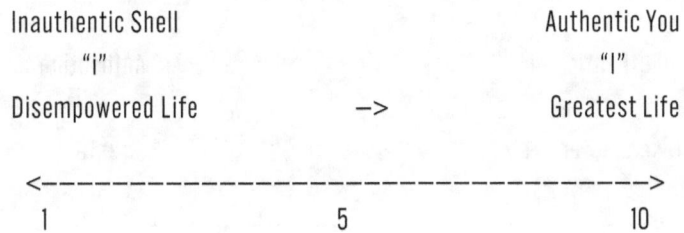

Your life is spacious and light.

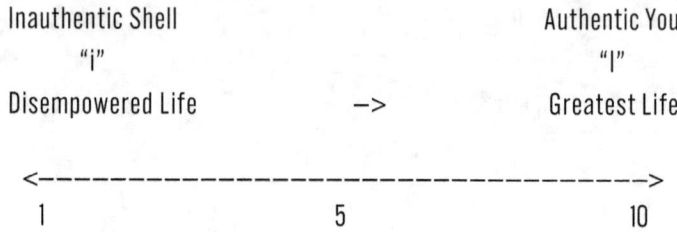

Your well-being becomes a natural state . . . not something you need to work at.

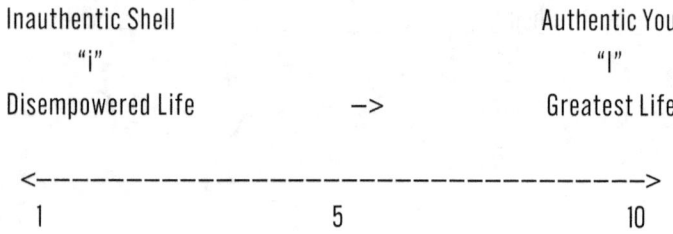

Your inner discomfort or pain that drove your compulsive behavior is gone.

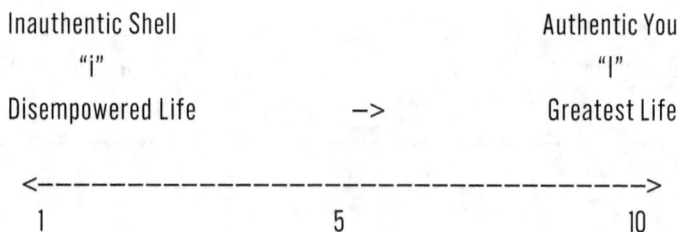

You enjoy peace and quiet.

Inauthentic Shell   Authentic You
    "i"   "I"
Disempowered Life   –>   Greatest Life

<----------------------------------->
1   5   10

Your energy increases dramatically.

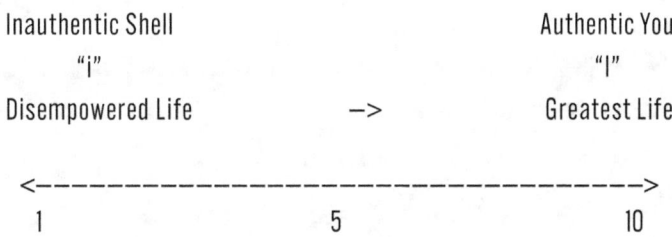

Inauthentic Shell   Authentic You
    "i"   "I"
Disempowered Life   –>   Greatest Life

<----------------------------------->
1   5   10

You have a deep sense of power you've never felt before.

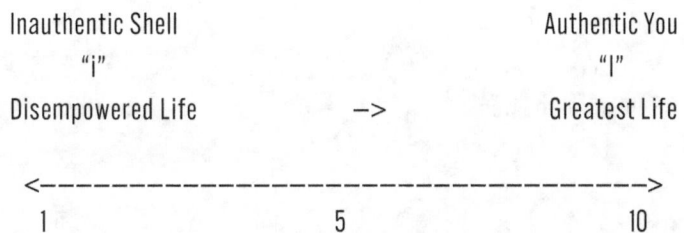

Inauthentic Shell   Authentic You
    "i"   "I"
Disempowered Life   –>   Greatest Life

<----------------------------------->
1   5   10

You have a personal connection with your Inner Power.

Inauthentic Shell   Authentic You
    "i"   "I"
Disempowered Life   ->   Greatest Life

<----------------------------------->
1   5   10

You trust and follow your Inner Guidance.

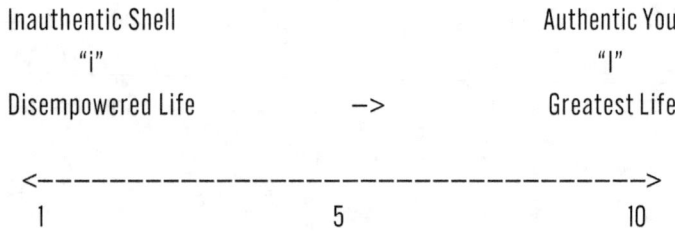

You don't need the approval from others.

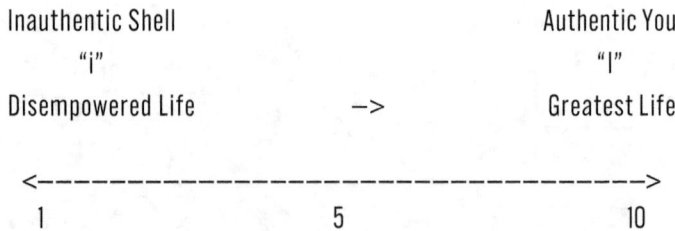

You feel empowered . . . you're no longer a victim of life.

Inauthentic Shell   Authentic You
     "i"   "I"
Disempowered Life   ->   Greatest Life

<----------------------------------->
1   5   10

You are committed to your life's purpose . . . something much greater than just yourself.

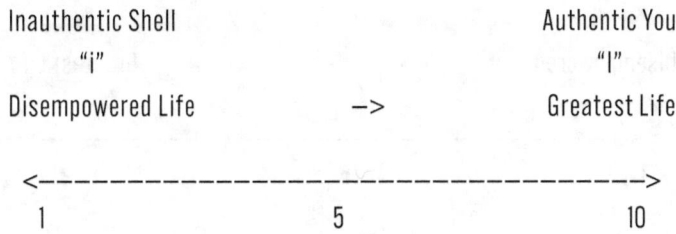

Inauthentic Shell   Authentic You
     "i"   "I"
Disempowered Life   ->   Greatest Life

<----------------------------------->
1   5   10

Your creativity has been empowered.

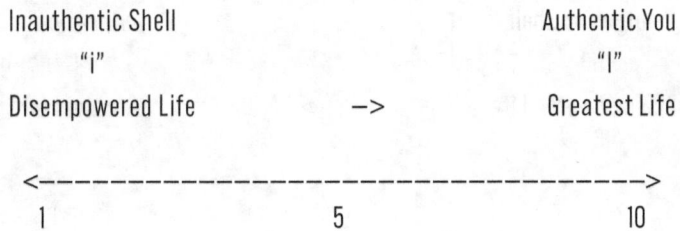

Inauthentic Shell   Authentic You
     "i"   "I"
Disempowered Life   ->   Greatest Life

<----------------------------------->
1   5   10

Your life is created . . . inside-out.

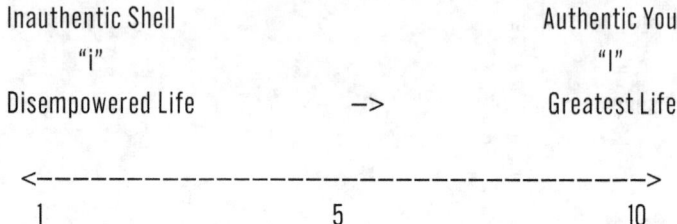

Taking personal responsibility is easy and natural.

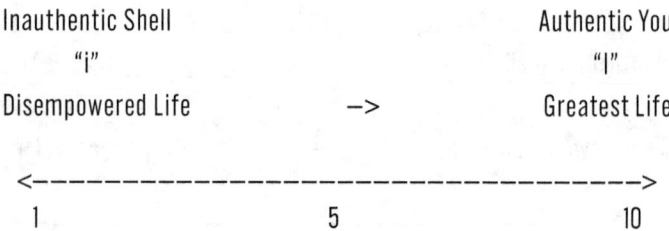

You look at what might go right in life . . . as opposed to what might go wrong.

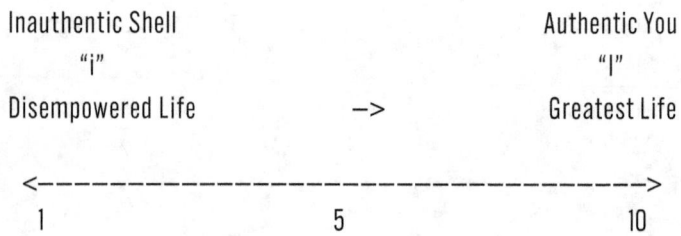

Your life becomes more about contribution, adventure, experiences, and people . . . rather than the accumulation of stuff.

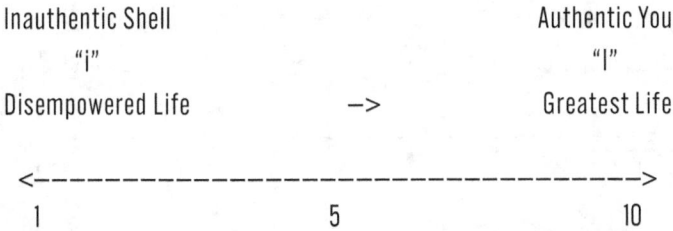

Life becomes your playground.

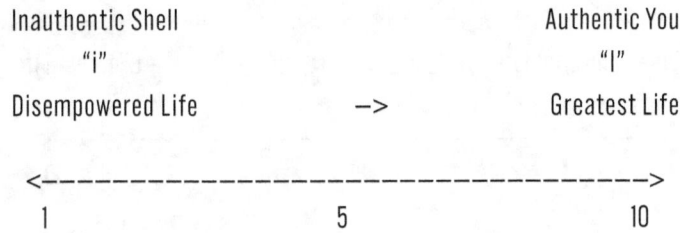

Retirement is no longer the goal; living a purposeful and passionate life is.

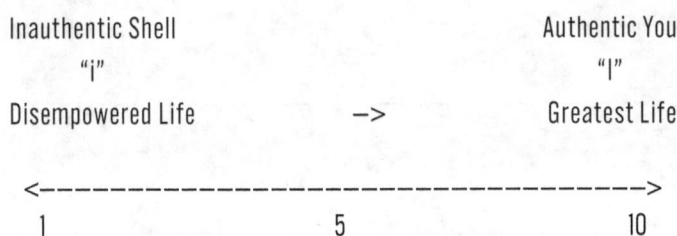

You feel connected with life.

Inauthentic Shell   Authentic You
"i"   "I"
Disempowered Life   ->   Greatest Life

<----------------------------------->
1   5   10

You feel a oneness . . . with all life.

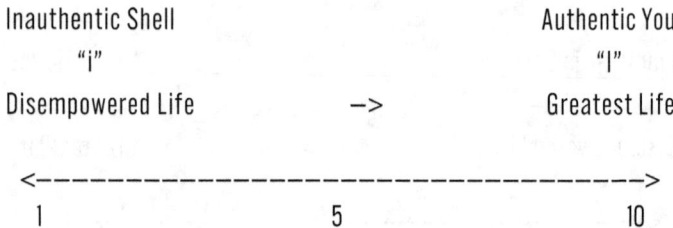

You naturally want to create a better world.

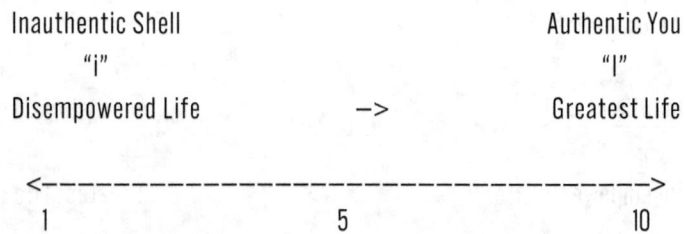

*For a downloadable "The Transformed You" Assessment, go to FreerJourney.com/The-Transformed-You-Assessment

APPENDIX C:
I-LIGNMENT MEDITATION AND RELEASE TECHNIQUES

POWERFUL TOOLS FOR TRANSFORMATION

MEDITATION

The Mayo Clinic's portrayal of meditation:

*"Meditation, a type of mind-body medicine, has
been practiced for thousands of years. During
meditation, you develop intentional focus—
minimizing random thoughts about the past or
future. Many forms of meditation exist, but most
have in common a quiet setting, a comfortable
position, focused attention, and an open attitude.
Meditation may offer many benefits, such as
helping with concentration, relaxation, inner
peace, stress reduction . . ."*

Meditation is a powerful tool to embrace and use for enhancing your overall well-being . . . as well as transforming your life.

There are three primary roles meditation plays in the I-Lignment process. First, meditation brings all your attention to the present moment, quieting the mind, and creating a calm space. As you now know, this is critical because the now is the only place you can start and continue your transformational journey inward. Second, meditation allows the discomfort in your life (inhibiting emotions, thoughts, beliefs, and stories) to rise into your awareness in this calm space to be clearly seen and heard . . . and then released. This releasing reduces the thickness and density of your shell and, over time, dissipates it, allowing you to go beyond it inward to be in and live from your "I"ntersection . . . "I." Third, meditation creates the inner quiet so you can hear and follow your Inner Guidance . . . critical to living an authentic life inside-out.

I-LIGNMENT MEDITATION AND RELEASE TECHNIQUES

There are literally hundreds of ways to meditate and release. Seven techniques will be introduced and used during the I-Lignment process. These specific techniques are used because they're easily incorporated into your everyday life. You can use them anytime, anywhere . . . even when you're talking with other people. This is important because life doesn't wait for formal meditation sessions to trigger you; it happens whenever and wherever.

The meditations used to help prepare you for your transformational journey inward are:

- "Be Present" Meditation
- "Be Present to Inner Awareness" Meditation
- "Be Present to Your True Self" Meditation

Once you're prepared, there are release techniques that are used during I-Lignment on your inward journey.

- "i-Release" Release Technique
- "The Why" Release Technique
- "I-Flow" Release Technique
- "I-Forgive" Release Technique

Each of these meditations and release techniques are described in this appendix.

A WAY OF LIFE

The initial structured meditation sessions each day, as part of your Empowering the "I"ntersection routine, are intended to develop the "muscle" to effectively use meditation and release as transformative tools and to work through the focused release of more difficult parts of your shell. As you practice and become proficient during these dedicated times, they then evolve into tools you can use anytime you need them throughout your day.

After you significantly decrease the power of the contents of your shell over your life and begin living a life from the inside-out, meditation and release then shift to tools of maintenance, keeping you in flow from the inside-out and stopping the reestablishment of a rigid, time-based shell.

They enable you to show up in each moment powerfully and authentically . . . being present . . . being in presence . . . being in peace . . . being in love . . . always.

NOTE: This is an effective thing I say to myself periodically throughout the day, "Be present . . . be in presence . . . be in peace . . . be in love . . . always." If I feel those four things are happening, then I go about my day knowing I'm living life from the right place. If I know it's not happening, then I use meditation and release to help put me back into that state.

BE PRESENT

I-LIGNMENT MEDITATION TECHNIQUE

The "Be Present" meditation's main purpose is to bring you into the present moment, quiet the mind, and create a calm, peaceful space. It's the beginning point of your transformation and is the foundation for all the other meditation and release techniques.

Being present can be realized by solely focusing on anything with you in the moment that you begin meditation. It could be a focus on a tree, flower, table . . . anything. However, your breath is what is used in this technique, because it's always with you. Breath is never in the past or future; it's only in the present. At any time and place, you can focus on your breath and bring yourself present to create a calm, still, and quiet space.

By doing a minimum of fifteen minutes of the "Be Present" meditation in the morning and fifteen minutes in the evening before bed, you'll gain experience in its use, and this will evolve into a habit of staying present as a way of life as you extend it into the rest of your day.

Preparing for Meditation

The following are things you can do to prepare for meditation to make it most effective.

- Find a quiet spot where you'll have privacy. It's best to use the same spot so you can develop a consistent routine. Ideally, it's somewhere that inspires you.
- Make sure the space is at a temperature that feels comfortable.
- If it calms you, put peaceful, nonvocal music on at a low volume in the background.
- Choose to meditate by sitting upright or lying horizontal. If you're lying down, put something under

your knees and under your head to reduce any strain in your body.

- Commit to your meditation routine no matter what. This can't be overemphasized. The "Be Present" meditation will empower your escape from your time-based mind, which is constantly trying to pull you back into the past and future. By being consistent, you'll develop your "muscle" to break free.

- Keep it simple . . . don't overcomplicate it. Just focus on being present. Don't have any expectations of anything else happening.

- Expect inner resistance, especially at the beginning. Your mind, which always wants to be actively thinking about the past or future, will do everything it can to pull you out of any attempt to be present. This resistance can show up in many ways physically, mentally, and emotionally, such as being too tired, getting sick, getting angry about the process, or getting too busy. You just need to push through this resistance by consistently doing the meditation. The only way is through.

"Be Present" Meditation Process . . .

Settle into a position that will allow you to stay as still as possible during the entire meditation . . . then close your eyes.

Begin by focusing on your continuous, natural breathing . . . focus on both the in breath and out breath . . . keep your concentrated focus on just your breath, breathing through either your nose or mouth.

If thoughts come into your mind, don't focus on them . . .

give them the label "thinking" and then let them float on by . . . then bring your attention back to your breathing only.

Enjoy the stillness, calm, and peace you're experiencing . . . by just being present . . . be in this state for the rest of the meditation.

Before ending the meditation, set an intention that you'll maintain this state of being present from this point forward.

Gradually come out of the meditation when you're ready. Open your eyes . . . be open and receptive to everything going on around you just as it is . . . right now . . . in this present moment.

NOTE: You can listen to a coach-guided, audio recording of this I-Lignment meditation technique at FreerJourney. com/Be-Present.

BE PRESENT TO INNER AWARENESS

I-LIGNMENT MEDITATION TECHNIQUE

This meditation is a process for increasing your awareness of your inner life . . . your body sensations, emotions, thoughts, beliefs, and stories. This is a must if you're to be successful in dissipating your shell on your inner journey to "I" and then creating your Greatest Life. You can't resolve what you don't know exists.

As you meditate, pay attention to both the obvious emotions, beliefs, and stories, as well as the more subtle ones. Have a paper and pen ready to capture them as they arise. Keep the notes brief. Once you capture them on paper, quickly resume the meditation. If you can, however, it's best to wait until the end to capture what comes up so you don't disrupt being fully engaged in the meditation.

"Be Present to Inner Awareness" Meditation Process...

Settle into a position that will allow you to stay as still as possible during the entire meditation . . . then close your eyes.

Begin by focusing on your continuous, natural breathing . . . focus on both the in breath and out breath . . . keep your concentrated focus on just your breath, breathing through either your nose or mouth.

If thoughts come into your mind, don't focus on them . . . give them the label "thinking" and then let them float on by . . . then bring your attention back to your breathing only.

Enjoy the stillness, calm, and peace you're experiencing . . . by just being present . . . stay in this state for the rest of the meditation.

In this calm and quiet, now allow all your senses to fully open . . . increase the sensitivity of your hearing . . . of your smelling . . . your ability to taste . . . your seeing . . . sensations all over your skin.

Sense what's happening around you . . . feel the air flowing past you . . . the heat or cold . . . sense any movement in the room around you . . . the sounds coming to you . . . the smells in the room.

Feel yourself being receptive to all that you're sensing externally and will soon be experiencing internally . . . allowing everything to be just as it is . . . without thinking . . . not needing anything to be other than what it is in this moment . . . simply allowing things to happen naturally just as they are.

Now shift your attention inward . . . you're going to be increasing your inner awareness by rotating your attention throughout your body.

Begin by bringing your attention to the top of your head . . . feel the sensations of your scalp under your hair all over your skull.

Now focus on your face, noticing any sensations in your forehead . . . eyes . . . nose . . . cheeks . . . jaw . . . the skin of your face . . . tighten your entire face and then release the tension . . . feel your face relax . . . open your mouth . . . and stick out your tongue as far as you can . . . feel the tension in your mouth and tongue . . . release the tension . . . wiggle your head, mouth, and jaw and then allow them to relax . . . feel the sensations that remain.

Sense sounds coming to your ears . . . creating vibrations in your eardrum.

Feel any tension or discomfort in your neck and shoulders . . . tighten your neck and shoulders for a few moments and then release . . . rotate your head and neck around in both directions . . . then shake your head and shoulders around . . . relax them both completely . . . feel the sensations now.

Slide your awareness down into your chest area . . . create tension in your chest muscles and your upper back . . . hold both for several seconds and then release . . . In your chest, feel the sensations on your skin, in your muscles, and in the inner cavity of your chest . . . feel your heart as it beats . . . sense any tension or discomfort . . . feel the rise and fall of your lungs as you breathe . . . notice if your breathing is rhythmic and relaxed or uneven and restricted . . . notice if you breathe deep or shallow . . . do all of this without judgment . . . with total acceptance of what is happening right now.

Notice the sensations in your right arm . . . wiggle the fingers in your right hand and then curl them into a fist . . . tighten the fist and, as you do, allow that tension in your hand to create tension throughout your arm . . . from your wrist to your forearm . . . then your elbow . . . biceps . . . triceps. Tighten the arm as hard as you can . . . and then release the tension . . . shake it . . . and relax it completely . . . notice the sensations in that arm now.

Now feel the sensations in your left arm . . . wiggle the fingers in your left hand and then curl them into a fist . . . tighten the fist and, as you do, allow that tension in your hand to create tension throughout your arm . . . from your wrist to your forearm . . . then your elbow . . . biceps . . . triceps. Tighten the arm as hard as you can . . . and then release the tension . . . shake it . . . and relax it completely . . . notice the sensations in that arm now.

Feel the heightened awareness of the sensations now in your chest . . . in your shoulders and arms . . . in your neck . . . in your face . . . in your ears . . . around your head.

Tighten your stomach muscles and then relax them . . . tighten your middle and lower back muscles and then relax them . . . notice the sensations in your spine and back muscles . . . notice the sensations in your abdomen organs, noticing any discomfort . . . in your stomach . . . in your liver . . . in your intestines . . . in your bladder . . . in your sexual organs . . . don't label them good or bad, just notice the sensations. Feel where the most intense sensation is.

Shift your focus to your pelvic area . . . create tension

in the pelvic muscles and butt cheeks . . . hold that tension tight for a moment and then release it . . . feel the sensations in this area now . . . in the muscles . . . in the lower spine.

Bring your awareness now to your right thigh . . . then to the knee . . . calf . . . ankle . . . foot . . . and then toes . . . tighten your entire leg and then release it and completely relax it . . . feel the sensations in your right leg now.

Bring your awareness now to your left thigh . . . then to the knee . . . calf . . . ankle . . . foot . . . and then toes . . . tighten your entire leg and then release it . . . completely relax it . . . now feel the sensations in your left leg.

Now tense your whole body, making every part . . . every muscle . . . tight and straining . . . then completely release all tension. Feel your body alive now, radiating with sensation . . . feel how aware you are of all the sensations now . . . realize the sensations are right here, right now . . . not in the distant past or future.

Notice where your awareness is naturally drawn to in your body . . . to a sensation that needs attention . . . feel that sensation . . . welcome it . . . and allow it to be whatever it wants to be in that moment . . . know it is meant to be here and is asking for your attention.

Is there an emotion attached to the sensation . . . if so, what is the emotion? . . . allow yourself to really feel and experience the emotion . . . then ask what it's trying to tell you. Is there an underlying belief or story that has caused the emotion? What is it?

Continue to notice where your awareness is drawn to other sensations in your body . . . and their related emotions, thoughts, beliefs, or stories. Continue to do this as new sensations come up.

Before ending the meditation, recommit to your intention that you'll maintain this state of being present from this point forward . . . and commit to having greater awareness of your inner state . . . being more aware of the sensations, emotions, thoughts, beliefs, and stories you're experiencing in each moment.

Gradually come out of the meditation when you're ready . . . open your eyes . . . be open and receptive to everything going on around you and within you . . . right now . . . in this present moment.

> NOTE: You can listen to a coach-guided audio recording of this I-Lignment meditation technique at FreerJourney.com/Inner-Awareness.

BE PRESENT TO YOUR TRUE SELF

I-LIGNMENT MEDITATION TECHNIQUE

This meditation leads you to an awareness and experience of your true self, your authentic "I," separate from your shell. This is an important tool of your inner journey to "I"; it creates the conditions for you to release your shell bit by bit with minimal inner resistance.

"Be Present to Your True Self" Meditation Process . . .

Settle into a position that will allow you to stay as still as possible during the entire meditation . . . then close your eyes.

Begin by focusing on your continuous, natural breathing . . . focus on both the in breath and out breath . . . keep your concentrated focus on just your breath, breathing through either your nose or mouth.

If thoughts come into your mind, don't focus on them . . . give them the label "thinking" and then let them float on by . . . then bring your attention back to your breathing only.

Enjoy the stillness, calm, and peace you're experiencing . . . by just being present . . . be in this state for the rest of the meditation.

From this state of quiet and calm, begin to rotate your awareness throughout your body . . . and do so without any judgment . . . only observing what is happening in this moment in your body.

Feel the sensations . . . in your head . . . on your scalp . . . on your forehead . . . in your eyes . . . on and in your nose . . . your ears . . . your lips . . . your tongue . . . your teeth and gums . . . your jaw . . . your chin. Create tension in your entire face . . . and then release it. Be aware of all the sensations now throughout your head.

Shift your awareness to your neck . . . feel the sensations in your throat . . . in the muscles of your neck . . . in your spine . . . bring tension to your entire neck . . . and then release it. Be aware of all the sensations now in your neck.

Drop your awareness into your chest . . . sense the rise and fall of your chest as you breathe . . . feel the air rush into your lungs and then back out again . . . notice if your breathing is easy or constricted. Feel your heart beating rhythmically. Bring your attention to the muscles in your chest . . . then your upper back . . . then your shoulders . . . notice if they're tight or relaxed . . . bring tension to your entire chest, shoulders, and upper back . . . and then release it. Be aware of all the sensations now throughout your upper body.

Bring your awareness to your right arm . . . your biceps . . . your elbow . . . your forearm . . . wrist . . . hand . . . fingers. Curl your hand into a fist . . . then, from there, tighten your entire right arm to your shoulder . . . and then release it. Be aware of the remaining sensations in your arm.

Bring your awareness to your left arm . . . your biceps . . . your elbow . . . your forearm . . . wrist . . . hand . . . fingers. Curl your hand into a fist . . . then, from there, tighten your entire left arm to your shoulder . . . and then release it. Be aware of the remaining sensations in that arm.

Lower your awareness into your abdomen . . . feeling the sensations in your liver . . . stomach . . . intestines . . . pancreas . . . bladder . . . sexual organs . . . lower back. Tighten the muscles in your lower back and abdomen at the same time . . . and release. Be aware of the sensations now.

Focus your awareness on both legs and your pelvic area at the same time . . . feel the sensations throughout that area . . . bring tension to both legs, feet, and the pelvic area at the same time and hold it . . . then release. Be aware of the remaining sensations.

Now bring your awareness to what emotions are in your body . . . observe where they're showing up in the form of sensations such as tension, pain, discomfort . . . or warmth, peacefulness, love. Identify, if you can, what the emotions are.

Now allow your awareness to uncover the thoughts, beliefs, or stories behind each emotion . . . be aware of other thoughts, beliefs, and stories swirling around in your mind.

Expand your awareness to encompass all the sensations you've been experiencing throughout your body . . . the emotions you've identified, and the thoughts, beliefs, and stories you've uncovered.

Notice your awareness lies outside of it all . . . realize if your awareness was part of your body/sensations/emotions/mind, you wouldn't be able to "stand back" and observe them. With this new insight, feel your awareness expand beyond your body . . . then "look back" from a distance. This helps you clearly see you are not trapped in your body . . . in your emotions . . . in your mind of the remembered past and restricted future. They're not who you are in truth . . . they are part of your inauthentic self, created from the outside-in. Who you are in truth is this "I" that is observing it all . . . feel the freedom . . . the spaciousness . . . the vastness . . . that you get from this realization . . . feel how it opens you up to unlimited possibilities in your life . . . how you fall into a deep sense of peace.

For the rest of the meditation, continue to experience this new awareness that you are separate from what you thought was "you" . . . that it really is an inauthentic self, created from the outside-in . . . and that you've discovered your authentic "I."

Before ending the meditation, recommit to your intention you'll maintain this state of "being present" from this point forward . . . commit to living from the new awareness that you are much greater than your current shell . . . knowing that your authentic "I" is at your core where you can experience true individual freedom, unconditional love, deep peace, constant contentment, and an underlying joy . . . knowing this is the only source for creating your Greatest Life.

Gradually come out of the meditation when you're ready . . . open your eyes . . . be open and receptive to everything going on around you and within you . . . right now . . . in this present moment.

> NOTE: You can listen to a coach-guided audio recording of this I-Lignment meditation technique at FreerJourney. com/True-Self.

I-RELEASE

I-LIGNMENT RELEASE TECHNIQUE

i-Release is a powerful tool to use throughout your transformational journey. It's highly effective at dissipating your shell. If you learned only one release tool, this is the one to master. Don't underestimate its power to release and transform.

The power lies in the ability to use it anytime, anywhere . . . even when you're talking with another person. It allows you to welcome the inhibiting emotions and beliefs that bubble to the surface in everyday life at the time they occur, hear what they're here to tell you, and then to release them immediately. You can quickly reduce the impact of the emotion or belief as they're affecting you in that moment. Not only does it reduce the intensity of the emotion/belief and release it, but it also stops negative thoughts from spinning out of control before they even begin.

At the beginning, use it during the daily meditation and release sessions to practice it and see its effective results. However, you want to quickly get to the point where you can use it lying down, sitting, standing, or walking . . . so it can be used throughout the day . . . and night.

i-Release Release Meditation . . .

When you start feeling an inhibiting emotion being triggered, quickly bring yourself present by focusing on your breathing. Then go inside and identify where in your body you're specifically feeling it. Allow the emotion to be whatever it wants to be in that moment. With your focus on it, it may increase in intensity; let it. It may move around in your body; follow it. You want to have minimum resistance to it, so it hangs around until you hear its message and are then able to release it.

Go to the most intense center of the emotion.

Welcome it. Invite it, metaphorically, into your home for a cup of tea and conversation. Ask it what it's here to tell you. In doing this, you're looking for a possible underlying cause of the emotion. You may hear the "message" in that moment . . . perhaps it's a limiting belief like "I'm not good enough." You may also not hear a message but just experience the emotion. In either case, you release on one or both.

Once you listen to the emotion, you can then release it. The i-Release process is like peeling the layers of an onion. You take one layer off, and it gets smaller. You take the next layer off, and it gets even smaller. If done enough times, the onion eventually is gone. The same happens to your emotion and underlying belief.

Follow these steps:

1. Ask yourself, "Do I want to release it now?"
2. If you do, say "Yes."
3. Then release it. You'll feel the energy of the emotion

flowing out through your body, legs, and feet, or through your body, arms, and hands.

4. You then go back to the emotion and see if it still exists. If it does, you continue to repeat steps one through four until the emotion is gone.

5. If you've heard a message associated with the emotion, an underlying belief, then you can go through the same steps to release it.

It's a simple process. That's what makes it so powerful. Over time, you no longer need to ask the questions, but, rather, you just feel the emotion or belief and then release it . . . over and over until it's gone.

Once it's gone, the result is a feeling of peace and spaciousness where there was once dis-ease and denseness. If you use i-Release consistently, you *will* dissipate your shell.

NOTE: You can listen to a coach-guided audio recording of this I-Lignment release technique at FreerJourney. com/i-Release.

THE WHY

I-LIGNMENT RELEASE TECHNIQUE

The "Big Why" was introduced earlier, as part of your I-Lignment journey, to create a powerful personal motivation for transformational change . . . creating massive pain with staying the way you are and massive pleasure with going through the transformation to realize your Greatest Life. People will go to great lengths to avoid pain and will do the same to gain something in their life that gives them feelings of pleasure and achieving something much grander than what they have. So, if you want to create powerful motivation to initiate and achieve changes in your life, you need to associate massive pain with staying the same and associate massive pleasure and gain with changing. To create the most powerful motivation for change, you need to do both. The pain will push you to action . . . and the pleasurable gain will pull you to action.

The same concept can be applied to individual inhibiting emotions and beliefs. During this process, you once again associate massive pain with having them remain in your life and massive pleasure with having them transform into something different that is I-Ligned with your Greatest Life.

"The Why" Release Meditation . . .

Settle into a position that will allow you to stay as still as possible during the entire meditation . . . then close your eyes.

Begin by focusing on your continuous, natural breathing . . . focus on both the in breath and out breath . . . keep your concentrated focus on just your breath, breathing through either your nose or mouth.

If thoughts come into your mind, don't focus on them . . . give them the label "thinking" and then let them float on by . . . then bring your attention back to your breathing only.

Enjoy the stillness, calm, and peace you're experiencing . . . by just being present.

Now feel an inhibiting emotion or belief being triggered

in you. Go inside and identify where in your body you're specifically feeling it. Allow the emotion/belief to be whatever it wants to be in that moment. With your focus on it, it may increase in intensity; let it. It may move around in your body; follow it. You want to have minimum resistance to it, so it hangs around until you hear its message and are then able to release it. Go to the most intense center of the emotion/belief.

Now begin the process of creating a powerful "Why" for transforming the emotion/belief.

Create massive "pain" associated with the emotion/belief. Really "see" the impact of this emotion/belief in your life. Realize how you've been negatively impacted in the past and present. See how it's hurt the people you love. Feel the dysfunction you've brought into your life and the world around you. Feel the pain. Feel it deeply. Experience the pain with all your senses . . . see it, feel it, hear it, smell it, taste it. Look forward five years in the future. See it continuing to have the same or worse impact on your life. See it impacting how you see yourself and how others see you. Think about everything you have lost by having it. Imagine even more pain inflicted on yourself and the people you care about. Then project it out even further . . . ten years . . . twenty years . . . and go through the same process. See your quality of life continuing to painfully deteriorate.

Do you really want to continue to have this emotion/belief? Do you want to continue to have this pain?

Shout . . . Nooooooo!

Envision a life without the emotion/belief. Replace it with an emotion/belief that is more empowering. See how life could be so much better if you felt or believed differently. Allow this new emotion/belief and new way of living life to flow from deep inside of you; allow it to unfold from the inside-out. Put yourself into this new life as if it's happening right now.

See it, feel it, hear it, smell it, taste it. Envision how much more beautiful your life would be . . . more peaceful . . . more loving . . . more joyful . . . more free . . . more motivating . . . more energizing . . . much more powerful.

Shout "Yes" to this new way of living life!

You're now empowered with "The Why" . . . you clearly see current emotion/belief is unacceptable in your life . . . and you also have a clear picture of an amazing life that results from replacing it.

Before ending the meditation, set an intention you'll only live with the new empowering emotion/belief from this point forward.

Gradually come out of the meditation when you're ready. Open your eyes . . . be open and receptive to everything going on around you just as it is . . . right now . . . in this present moment.

NOTE: You can listen to a coach-guided audio recording of this I-Lignment release technique at FreerJourney.com/ The-Why.

I-FLOW

I-LIGNMENT RELEASE TECHNIQUE

"I-Flow" is a powerful release technique most effectively

used once you have shifted, at least partially, to your Inner Source of Life and its unlimited supply of unconditional love. The power of love is expressed in many ways, by many cultures and religions, and by the saying, "Love conquers all." Its power is recognized and understood. Unconditional love, as one of the most powerful energies, has the capacity to dissolve virtually any other lower-level energy (emotion, belief) given enough repetition.

Using the flow of love energy throughout your body will cleanse you of emotional impurities of lower-level energies. By using I-Flow as a release technique, you're dissolving parts of your shell while, at the same time, allowing yourself to increasingly experience love at each step of your I-Lignment journey. Eventually unconditional love remains . . . one of the natural outcomes of finally arriving at your "I"ntersection. At "I," you become unconditional love.

There are two variations of this release technique:

Variation 1: Flowing unconditional love from the top of the head as a powerful river of love . . . down through the body and out the hands and feet . . . dissolving lower-level energies as it goes.

Variation 2: Flowing unconditional love from your heart, imagining your heart as an infinite inner spring of love, then flowing it in all directions throughout your body . . . then out every pore of your body and into everything around you . . . dissolving the lower-level energies as it goes.

You can use the variation that feels most right for you. Or use both.

"I-Flow" Release Meditation: Love through Your Body

Settle into a position that will allow you to stay as still as possible during the entire meditation . . . then close your eyes.

Begin by focusing on your continuous, natural breathing . . . focus on both the in breath and out breath . . . keep your concentrated focus on just your breath, breathing through either your nose or mouth.

If thoughts come into your mind, don't focus on them . . . give them the label "thinking" and then let them float on by . . . this way you release any attachment or importance to the thought in that moment . . . then bring your attention back to your breathing only.

Enjoy the stillness, calm, and peace you're experiencing . . . by just being present.

Now imagine there is a powerful, yet peaceful, river of love flowing into the crown of your head from an unlimited love spring. As it flows down your body, see it flowing into and filling every part of your body . . . every cell . . . infusing everything with powerful love. Feel it flowing into your head . . . down your neck . . . into your shoulders and upper back . . . down your arms . . . then out through your hands. Feel it continue down into your chest . . . down into your abdomen and lower back . . . then hips . . . down both legs . . . then out of your body through your feet. The flow is strong and constant, yet gentle.

As it flows past and around the inhibiting emotions you're feeling in your body, imagine the emotions starting to erode in the power of the current. Allow love to continue to flow around the emotions, dissolving them bit by bit by bit . . . getting smaller and smaller . . . until they completely dissolve into the love that flows around them.

Relish the love that remains.

Before ending the meditation, set an intention you'll maintain this state of "being in love" from this point forward.

Gradually come out of the meditation when you're ready. Open your eyes . . . be open and receptive to everything going on around you just as it is . . . right now . . . in this present moment.

> NOTE: Your can listen to a coach-guided audio recording of this I-Lignment release technique at FreerJourney. com/I-Flow-Body.

———

"I-Flow" Release Meditation: Love from Your Heart

Settle into a position that will allow you to stay as still as possible during the entire meditation . . . then close your eyes.

Begin by focusing on your continuous, natural breathing . . . focus on both the in breath and out breath . . . keep your concentrated focus on just your breath, breathing through either your nose or mouth.

If thoughts come into your mind, don't focus on them . . . give them the label "thinking" and then let them float on by . . . then bring your attention back to your breathing only.

Enjoy the stillness, calm, and peace you're experiencing . . . by just being present.

Now imagine love flowing from an infinite, inner spring into your heart. Feel it flowing out of your heart in all directions . . . filling your chest with unconditional love . . . then up into your shoulders, neck, and head . . . down into your arms and hands . . . flowing down into your abdomen, hips . . . then your legs and feet. Feel your body being fully infused with love . . . in every part . . . in every organ . . . in every cell. Feel it flowing out of every pore of your skin into the world around you . . . filling the world around you with love.

As it flows past and around any inhibiting emotions you're feeling in your body, imagine the emotions starting to dissolve in the power of the love. Like a sugar cube in hot water, feel them getting smaller and smaller . . . until they completely dissolve into the love that flows around them.

Relish in the love that remains.

Before ending the meditation, set an intention you'll maintain this state of "being in love" from this point forward.

Gradually come out of the meditation when you're ready. Open your eyes . . . be open and receptive to everything going on around you just as it is . . . right now . . . in this present moment.

NOTE: You can listen to a coach-guided audio recording of this I-Lignment release technique at FreerJourney. com/I-Flow-Heart.

"I-FORGIVE"

I-LIGNMENT RELEASE TECHNIQUE

"I-Forgive" is an incredibly powerful release technique as you react to difficult situations with people in your life. Forgiveness has the power to transform you, as part of your journey to the "I"ntersection, and the relationship with the other person at the same time . . . but only if you understand and use forgiveness correctly.

Forgiving in the way most of us do it is as a generous gift we bestow on others for things we perceive they've done wrong. They are beneficiaries of our generosity and kindness while, at the same time, we're still harboring the judgments against them. We've just pushed the judgments into the background of our mind . . . a form of coping. We have not really forgiven them.

True forgiveness begins when you know what was said or done by "them" is really a judgment (a belief) you have created in your mind and are projecting onto them. Through true forgiveness, you're releasing that judgment from your own mind independent of them and, therefore, releasing its impact on both them and (especially) you.

You also recognize the other person is living a life sourced from their inauthentic shell. They're living a life based on a dysfunctional, disjointed past created by others and filled with beliefs and emotional triggers with predictable reactions . . . just like the rest of us. This doesn't mean you condone their behavior, but rather you understand where their behavior is coming from. Through true forgiveness, you're looking past their inauthentic shell and recognizing their true "I."

With these two new perspectives, difficult relationships shift from being "bad" to now being an important part of your transformational journey. They are great reflections of what's going on inside of you; therefore, they become the messengers when they trigger you. The message is in the middle of the triggered reaction.

"I-Forgive" Release Meditation

Settle into a position that will allow you to stay as still as possible during the entire meditation . . . then close your eyes.

Begin by focusing on your continuous, natural breathing . . . focus on both the in breath and out breath . . . keep your concentrated focus on just your breath, breathing through either your nose or mouth.

If thoughts come into your mind, don't focus on them . . . give them the label "thinking" and then let them float on by . . . then bring your attention back to your breathing only.

Enjoy the stillness, calm, and peace you're experiencing . . . by just being present.

Now picture a difficult relationship in your life. Feel the emotions around that relationship and how they have been impacting both of your lives.

Now say the following words (in bold) silently to the other person:

"I'm sorry."

You're sorry for your misperception of seeing the other person as only their inauthentic shell, not who they are authentically. You're also sorry for projecting onto them your own internally triggered reaction.

"I forgive you."

By saying this, you're letting go of your judgment or

belief about them. Allow the judgment to flow out of you
. . . releasing part of your shell as you do.

"Please forgive me."

You're asking them to forgive you for your misperception.

"I love you unconditionally."

You love them unconditionally no matter what they think,
say, or do. Always being in the state of unconditional love is
one of the inherent attributes of "I"; this helps you reinforce
that attribute in yourself.

"Thank you."

You're feeling gratitude for this new way of relating to
others . . . knowing the relationship will be more authentic
from this point forward.

Even though the other person never hears what you say,
your forgiveness will transform the relationship. Most important, you're changing yourself first and, at the same time,
energetically sending forgiveness to the other person.

Before ending the meditation, set an intention you'll maintain this ability to "truly forgive" from this point forward.

Gradually come out of the meditation when you're ready.
Open your eyes . . . be open and receptive to everything
going on around you just as it is . . . right now . . . in this
present moment.

"Fear condemns . . . love forgives!!"

NOTE: You can listen to a coach-guided audio recording
of this I-Lignment release technique at FreerJourney.
com/I-Forgive.

322

APPENDIX D:
DYNAMIC POSSIBILITY EXAMPLE

RON MANSETH'S DYNAMIC POSSIBILITY

Be at the center of transformation . . . "I" . . . always!

Be the possibility of unconditional love, connectedness, and passion!

Be a transformational power in the world, helping people realize their Greatest Life . . . to live from their "I"ntersection, where they are infinitely authentic and powerful, where they can bring their purpose and possibility to the world!

Helping all of us to . . .
"Be Free—Live Free—Work Free"

Strong and profound connection with my Inner Source . . . God . . . in a way that allows cocreation in life . . . to provide powerful value to all around me and to all I touch in multiple ways.

Empowering the "I"ntersection daily. Living the states inherent at the "I"ntersection: free . . . loving . . . peaceful . . . content . . . joyful . . . passionate.

Focused on the process in each moment . . .

A life that demonstrates and is an example of a shift described in the I-Lignment book . . . driven by the internal connection and cocreation . . . an example of shift in perspective of what defines success . . . from big home, fancy car . . . to small, mobile, flexible, and supportive of the vision of a passionate life from within.

Positioned to go with the flow of life from within . . . able to pick up and change directions/locations easily to follow my Inner Guidance.

Bringing tremendous value to the world in general and to individual people specifically . . . helping people transform to their Greatest Life and to *Be Free*, *Live Free*, and *Work Free*. Accomplishing these things through businesses and initiatives that authentically transform lives.

Total mobility and flexibility to do my work wherever I am . . . with the infrastructure to support my work and pleasure . . . intermingled . . . worldwide . . . with everything online . . . no ties to any one location.

Outflows minimized and managed . . . inflows coming

from multiple sources and driven by my passions and focus on a prosperous life.

Great physical condition (energetic, great shape, flexible, relaxed) . . . working out consistently seven days/week . . . focused on my overall well-being.

Many rich and deep relationships around the world . . . people who are in alignment with spirit and values in the same way that I am.

Having a great relationship with my sons . . . loving and enjoying each other . . . having many experiences and adventures together.

Connoisseur of other cultures and geography . . . for personal interest, for business, for travels.

Gourmet cook . . . in general, soups, Thai, Indian, Japanese, dim sum, fondue, appetizers, sushi, barbecue.

Lots of adventures and experiences around the world and in the US.

Skilled traveler

Skilled backwoods hiker

Skilled snow skier

Skilled scuba diver

APPENDIX E:
ADDITIONAL RESOURCES

"Freer Journey" Blog

Weekly email messages will empower you on your I-Lignment journey and reinforce I-Ligning concepts as they apply to your life.

- Sign up at FreerJourney.com/home ... at the bottom of the webpage.

I-Lignment Coaching Programs and Retreats

I-Lignment individual and group coaching programs supplement and support the I-Lignment book.

- Explore the coaching offerings at FreerJourney.com/I-Lignment.

"Change Your World, Change The World" Movement!

Join forces with a growing group of people who are living in and from their authentic "I," realizing their Greatest Life, and having a powerful impact on the world.

- Join the movement at FreerJourney.com/ The-Movement.

ACKNOWLEDGMENTS

MANY PEOPLE IN my life have touched me to my very core and have taught me what an authentic relationship based on unconditional love really means. These relationships have been a shining light guiding me to the truth of life.

These people include my two sons, Erik Manseth and Jordan Manseth, and my nephew Andrew Manseth (whom I consider as one of my sons). I've loved them unconditionally their whole lives, and I can feel the unconditional love they radiate back . . . just because of who they are.

My mom, Anita McFarland, was one of the most giving, loving people I know. She was always there when any of us were in need, and she was always encouraging us to take risks and live our greatest lives. I appreciate her for all the love she showed and instilled in me from birth. I never doubted her love.

I learned gratitude for life from my grandmother Ester Manseth. She was grateful for even the simplest things and always looked on the bright side of life. She was a great example of what living in the present moment in love really means.

Aunt Donna Ambrose was one of my best friends. She taught me how to be there for others, listening to them without judgment, and loving them no matter what their life circumstances. She was a great example of unconditional love and true friendship.

My childhood friend Sue Hekimoglu has been a constant thread in my life since third grade. She has a huge heart and is constantly giving to others. I've been grateful for her loving friendship and unending support in both good times and bad.

I'd also like to greatly thank those people who helped bring the book to life: Celeste Mallett, who, as an energy coach, book reader/editor, and great friend, offered wise suggestions to improve the structure and content in the book; James Gallagher brought his professional editing skills to bear; and Kory Kirby put the book together to effectively and powerfully present the book to the world.

There are so many more friends, family, and colleagues I'd like to mention here and express my gratitude for their love, friendship, and contributions along my journey in life. You know who you are . . . and I love you all so much! Thank you for everything!

ABOUT THE AUTHOR

RON MANSETH IS the founder of Freer Journey™, an organization focused on empowering people feeling trapped by life to break free and create their Greatest Life . . . for the rest of their life.

As an author, coach, speaker, and entrepreneur, he has dedicated his life to help people powerfully transform their lives so they can live an authentic life on purpose and be empowered to bring their unique possibility to the world . . . in service of others.

He is also the founder and president of a business incubation coaching/consulting practice for developing and launching businesses that transform lives.